LEAD WITH A ME-SUITE MINDSET

OPTIONS ARE POWER

CAREER STRATEGIES FOR
HIGH PERFORMERS WHO WANT A LIFE

May you always have loads of options
- Donna

DONNA PETERS

Options Are Power

The contents of this book are for educational purposes only. Nothing contained herein should be construed as life advice or therapy, does not substitute for therapy if needed, and does not prevent, cure, or treat any mental disorder or medical disease. The information provided in this book is not a complete analysis of every material fact for any industry, business, or life situation. Opinions expressed are subject to change without notice.

Statements of fact cited have been obtained from sources considered reliable. No representation, however, is made as to the completeness or accuracy of any statement or data. This publication may include technical or other inaccuracies or typographical errors. Author assumes no responsibility for errors or omissions in this publication or other documents, which are referenced by or linked to this publication or the related website.

Nothing contained herein is, in any way, a guarantee or assurance that following strategies outlined in this book will create success or security, and readers should understand that they are responsible for the actions they take or do not take as a result of reading this book.

Donna Peters
The Me-Suite, LLC
The-Me-Suite.com

Published by
Elite Online Publishing
63 East 11400 South, Suite #230
Sandy, UT 84070
EliteOnlinePublishing.com

Library of Congress – In Progress
ISBN - 978-1-956642-01-8 (eBook)
ISBN - 978-1-956642-02-5 (Paperback)
ISBN - 978-1-956642-03-2 (Hardback)

Printed in the United States of America

FREE RESOURCE

I've interviewed over two hundred high-performing professionals as host of *The Me-Suite* podcast. There's a reason *The Me-Suite* was finalist for Best Business Podcast 2021 and Best Overall Podcast 2021[1]: the amazing guests. The guests span the dimensions of humanity and career diversity. While beautifully different in so many ways, these career-driven and life-minded guests are unified in their thoughtful pursuit of a career that serves the future they want.

Most of these conversations were recorded throughout the COVID-19 pandemic, making the timeliness of the discussions both eerie and energizing. The guests share themselves so fully at a time of great personal and societal reflection, the era being called the Great Resignation.

I've created a special podcast resource for readers of this book. With this free download, you'll receive *The Me-Suite Podcast Guest Guide*. This guide summarizes themes from the guest interviews across all seasons of *The Me-Suite* podcast. With the interactive guest guide, you can scan the diverse guests and topics to identify those of highest interest to you.

To download *The Me-Suite Podcast Guest Guide*,
scan the QR code or go to www.the-me-suite.com/guests.

[1] Kevin Goldberg, "Announcing the Winners of the 2021 Discover Pods Awards," https://awards.discoverpods.com/announcing-the-winners-of-the-2021-discover-pods-awards/, October 19, 2021.

For my mother, father, brother, and husband

who are all proof I won the family lottery.

Praises for Donna Peters

Donna Peters is an inspiration.

~Kerry Coffee, Founder and Principal, Schiller Discovery

Donna Peters is extremely thoughtful and brings a diverse set of experiences. Most importantly, she is honest and direct on what is needed to have a positive impact on your career and life.

~Dipak Patel, President and COO, Globo

Donna Peters is a trusted coach and brings a rare blend of business acumen, structured problem-solving, and listening skills, all wrapped up in a distinctly human and fun experience.

~Alan Nalle, Private Equity C-suite Leader

Donna's optimism, authenticity, and insight were a beacon for me. I recommend her and *The Me-Suite* for any professional seeking to rebalance career goals and amplify personal success.

~Donna Sanabria, VP, AstraZeneca

Donna opens your eyes to see things in a way you haven't seen them before.

~Colleen Pickett, VP, Takeda

Donna helped sharpen my narrative, which helped me meet my goal. She makes a difference.

~Amit Shah, Executive, Accenture

Donna's focus on values-driven leadership is strategic, goal-oriented, and actionable, delivering an exceptional and high-value experience.

~Fatima Sultan, VP, Vanguard

Donna's generative style and constant encouragement buoyed my first steps into a new iteration of my career. Donna's humor helped me smile, even when things were hard. She meets you where you are and helps you see your unique path forward.

~Sheryl Aikman, Founder, Alenda

Donna Peters is an effective and innovative executive coach. Thanks to her honest guidance, I was able to push my limits with confidence, discover my potential as a senior leader, and uncover pathways I had not thought of.

~A.S., Entrepreneurship and Innovation Leader

Donna Peters is a master of the art of guiding her clients through their goals and challenges and bringing out their individual motivation with intentional questions. She stays a step ahead, giving them room to come to the best conclusion for themselves and make strategic plans.

~Angelina Gurrola, Entrepreneur and Music Producer

Donna has a unique ability to encourage self-exploration from new perspectives. She helped me build a toolbox of invaluable skills.

~Alexander Idonije, Fulbright Scholar

Donna helped me feel prepared and confident in interviewing and navigating multiple offers. I strongly recommend Donna to anyone looking for professional support and guidance during a career transition.

~Alissa Twombly, Talent Development Consultant, EY

Working with Donna Peters is like having a smart, charismatic friend guide you through a maze she's already mastered. With the tremendous benefit of Donna's analytical and strategic thinking, I assessed competing visions of the second half of my career. Her genuine investment in my success was clear at every step.

~K.M., Lawyer

Contents

Foreword

It's worth reflecting on the vast number of times I have had a conversation with peers, team members, clients, and even family on this topic: how can I achieve the pinnacle of my career (whatever level that is) and have a life I cherish too? It's a big number because, at our core, this is the existential question we must all come face-to-face with on our journey.

I am grateful to have achieved both a wonderful family and work life. My amazing and truly better half of thirty years and I have raised two outstanding human beings, and along the way, I found myself advancing my roles and responsibilities at Accenture. It is a personal journey that has required courage, conviction, and colleagues like Donna to navigate.

Donna is among a handful of my most-valued confidantes on this topic. Together we've faced profoundly challenging business experiences while remaining true to our values and our commitments to our family and ourselves. In Donna, I have witnessed an admirable gift of being able to weave an intricately beautiful tapestry of both business and life. She brings her authentic self to every moment, and we are all the better for it.

I was privileged to serve on Donna's personal board of directors, advising her on the move from her inspiring career at Accenture to being the phenomenal founder of The Me-Suite. As I think about it now, once again, perhaps it was Donna who inspired me in those conversations.

In *Options Are Power*, Donna provides us with a toolkit for our personal and professional development. By opening this book, we open ourselves up to all the empowering options that lie ahead for each and every one of us. I can't imagine anyone better suited to help us build career strategies on our own terms.

~ Arjun Bedi, Senior Managing Director,
Global Management Committee Member, Accenture

CULTIVATE THE ROLE YOU WANT WORK TO PLAY IN YOUR LIFE

Lying atop a marginally comfortable bed in a Seattle hotel, wearing my Cornell sweatpants and allowing my laptop to live up to its name, I took a sip of the second nightly gin and tonic on the side table and ignored the TV as it blabbered some background local news. I had about three more hours of work to do for a client, and I was determined to finish before midnight. At seven p.m. on that fateful July night in 2010, my phone rang. It was Mom.

"Hi, shug. I have some troubling news," she said. "Your dad is having a heart attack." My mom was the leader of a high-pressure hospital laboratory. She had never been one to beat around the bush, but this level of bluntness was unusual, even for her.

"What? Is he okay?" I asked, not sure what else to say. As soon as I spoke the words, I realized how ridiculous they were. Of course he wasn't okay.

"He's in the hospital," she said.

My mind raced with options to address the issue at hand. I'm a natural problem solver, so I immediately went into fixer mode. "Do I need to come home?"

"Well, I know you're so busy," Mom replied empathetically, not actually answering my question. But the concern in her voice spoke for her. She needed me to be there.

"Let me check flights. I'm coming home."

The red-eye from Seattle to Birmingham via Atlanta allowed plenty of thinking time, maybe too much time. Not knowing whether my father would be alive on the other side, I checked my watch at least a dozen times during what seemed to be the longest flight I'd ever experienced from one coast to the other. I've since flown to South Africa and to Asia multiple times, both considerably more flight time than this one. Yet, that flight from the West Coast to the East Coast, with my dad's life in limbo, remains the longest flight I've ever taken.

Seated in an exit-row window, I listened as the pilots whispered updates. The flight attendants walked slowly through the aisle, in the dark, without the cart, scanning to make eye contact with anyone who might be awake. Back then, there wasn't Wi-Fi on planes, so red-eye flights were really dark and quiet. With sleep an impossibility for me, given the circumstances surrounding my trip, I kept my head down, trying to avoid eye contact with anyone, suspecting I'd start crying. Despite my efforts, I unintentionally caught a flight attendant's eyes as she passed my row.

"Can I get you anything, hon?"

Ugh! Too late to pretend my eyes are closed. "How about the snack box?" I mouthed this more than spoke it, making a square in the air with my fingers. She handed me the box I knew well from months flying this route. Oreos, cheese spread and crackers, and a mint. I stared out the window to the light at the end of the wing. It was following me like a personal moon. Helplessly, I wondered what was happening on the ground at UAB Medical Center. Was my father asking for me? Was he scared? I tried to recall the last thing I said to him. I knew it had been something pleasant. Our relationship was great, and I was grateful for that fact. But what had we last talked about? I couldn't remember. I wanted so badly to be there for him and Mom. If this was his last day, he'd be proud of his principled life and the family he had prioritized.

In contrast, I thought: *If this plane goes down and it's my last day, I'll be disappointed at best. If someone speaks at my funeral about my amazing abilities to build a merger integration playbook, I'm gonna be pissed. I'll be dead, of course, but I'll also be pissed.* In that moment, the reality of the life I had created reared its less-than-attractive head. I was doing everything in my power to get promoted as fast as I could. Work was working well. I was getting prime projects, accelerated promotions, high-profile task-force appointments. But on other dimensions, I wasn't doing so well. I'd gained about thirty pounds living on the road. My friendships were staler than rice cakes and just as bland. My husband saw me only two full days a week, and we spent much of that time together with our two friends, gin and tonic. My finances were fine, day to day, but not purposeful. I had quiet time in the air that night to think about my life.

The companies I most admired—Nike, Tesla, Johnson & Johnson, Accenture, Starbucks, Patagonia—all had core values that steered behavior, that took a stand, that created the future they wanted. I respected that. At the same time, like all high performers, these companies fell short of those core values from time to time. Whether due to an employee mix-up, the ill-spoken words of the CEO or board chair, faulty machinery, outdated processes, or some other faux pas, they screwed up. Only for them, the mess-ups landed front and center atop the headlines for the daily news rundown. Although not perfect, they had a clear North Star for quick course correction. *Why don't I have this steerage for my own life? What are my core values? How do my core values guide decisions for the future I want to live in?*

That red-eye flight was my moment that mattered. The moment I decided there is no work-life seesaw to balance. There is only my *life,* and all decisions I make, including those about work, must be in service of the life I want to live, not in balance with it.

Dad survived a widow-maker procedure while I was hurling at 35,000 feet with five hours of stress. Literally hurling. As a two-million-miler, my barf bag was typically used for stale chewing gum and trash, but this remains the only flight when I actually used the barf bag for barf.

When I entered his recovery room, Dad said, with a tired smile, "You didn't need to make this trip, doll. I know you're so busy."

Strange, I thought. *That's the same thing Mom said. Is that what my parents know most about me, that I'm busy?* In that moment, I decided no one I love would ever again feel I was too busy to show up. I decided I would make my career serve the life I wanted to live. Work would work for me. I also decided I didn't care too much for Oreos anymore.

I lived on the road, Monday through Thursday, as a management consultant for twenty years. My employers and my clients were and still are amazing companies with amazing humans doing amazing things to make the world a better place. Their C-suites, their most senior leaders, stay true to the core values and use those values to steer key decisions and make tough calls. They invest in their people to provide meaningful work in supportive cultures, and they steward important causes to shape a future that will make us all proud. I'd take the quiet time on the flight home Thursday nights to think about all I learned that week from my C-suite clients, chief ___ officers, and colleagues, the critical observations and lessons around ethics, innovation, branding, financial discipline, continuous learning, conflict resolution, the power of diversity, or how to give feedback.

For example, one week, I'd go deep in financials with a Chief Financial Officer (CFO) to understand the total cost of an investment decision. I used that learning in my own thought process for buying a home. Another week, I'd listen to customer feedback with a Chief Marketing Officer (CMO) to determine how best to differentiate a brand. I thought of my own brand on social media and how I needed a strategy for that. Some weeks I spent in R&D, focused on innovative ideas to keep the company competitive. I thought of my prediabetes blood work and how I needed to release Donna 4.0 and get back in shape.

Working with a Chief Operating Officer (COO) on supply chain challenges helped me see all the moving parts that must come together to deliver on promises. I thought of areas I could outsource to make things simpler at home. I learned the power of culture and communication from the M&A challenges faced by the Chief Strategy Officer (CSO) and head of Human Resources (CHRO). I thought of my family dynamics and culture, how we face conflict, what we talk about, what we don't, and why.

I helped a Chief Learning Officer (CLO) design the curriculum to teach old dogs new tricks in a digital economy. I thought of certifications I wanted to pursue and classes I wanted to take. The most impressive lessons of all were the discussions that happened at the most senior levels, in the C-suite, when core values were used to make decisions or address a crisis. I thought of my own core values, what they are, and why I had never thought about them before.

It always struck me as odd (and ironic and hypocritical and a little sad) that leaders get exposed to these amazing mindsets and disciplines for how to lead a company, but don't apply these mindsets and disciplines for leading their own lives. Work is an important part of life, but life should come first. Work is one decision high performers make about the life they want to live. Work isn't something to be balanced as an equal on a seesaw. Why, then, do more high performers not learn from and apply the examples of the C-suite companies they most admire to lead their own lives with more purpose, planning, and power? Couldn't all leaders be the CEO of their own life, have a CFO mindset to manage their financials, think like a Chief Marketing Officer to define the personal brand they want to have in the world, stay relevant for the future with a chief-learning-officer mindset, or chart their path with chief-strategy-officer discipline? Couldn't I?

On those late flights home, I had lots of quiet time for thinking. Well, maybe not so quiet. There was always some man snoring next to me, hogging space with his bear arm. Trying my best to ignore his breathing, in like a snort and out like a wee whistle, I drifted into "what if" scenarios. *What if I were in the C-suite? When I'm in the C-suite, I'll be more like so-and-so, less like so-and-so.* I started to think about what it would take to become like one of the C-suite leaders I most admired.

C-suite leaders have a tough job with awesome responsibility to get three things right:

1. Marshal the core values of the company.
2. Keep the day-to-day operations running smoothly.
3. Ensure the company stays fresh and relevant for the future.

Using my phone as a flashlight on the plane, and somewhat hoping the light would awaken the snoring bear, I wrote in my journal, "Why don't I take a C-suite approach to the way I lead my own personal life? I can recite the core values of my employer and client, but what are *my* core values? How am I keeping my day-to-day life running smoothly? How do I stay fresh and relevant for the future I want to have? I need a C-suite mindset for my own life." The questions flowed seamlessly, the answers far less. The reality that led to the Me-Suite concept didn't crystallize until that fateful night my mom called with the news about my dad. That changed everything—and I haven't looked back.

LEAD WITH A ME-SUITE MINDSET

My Aunt Nancy is a wonderful eighty-eight-year-old, wicked bright and full of *joie de vivre*. She would have been a psychologist had she grown up in a different era, and she is forever interested in everything I do. At my business launch celebration in 2020, she leaned over with her hearing aids buzzing and asked, "Donna, tell me, now. Why is your business called Sweet Me?"

Her innocence and curiosity tickled me. Never one to make light of a perfectly good question, I replied, smiling, "It's called The Me-Suite, Aunt Nancy. It's a play on the C-suite." I awaited her reply. When none came, I continued. "The C-suite are the most senior leaders in a company. The chiefs. Chief Executive Officer. Chief Financial Officer. The C stands for chief, and the suite is the group of chief executives that lead an organization. The C-suite. Does that make sense?"

With eyebrows raised and a bright smile accented with orange-red lipstick, she said, "I see. I don't think I knew that term."

With that, I felt the need to fill in the blanks a bit. "The Me-Suite believes individuals should lead their own personal lives with the same mindset that C-suites use to lead the companies we most admire. Having a Me-Suite mindset is a source of power for the career-oriented *and* life-minded person.

Aha! The lightbulb was turned on in that wicked sharp, eighty-eight-year-old brain. "Well, a Me-Suite sure sounds like a wise thing," she said. "You're still sweet to me."

Thanks to the influence of my parents, I have always been career oriented. My father owned a factory, where I grew up working on the shop floor, drill-pressing, staple-gunning, and sweeping sawdust. My mother worked full-time as an executive in health care. I knew very young that career would be a big part of my adult life. Indeed, I sought the fastest paths to promotion, doing whatever it took to grow into the next level of leadership. I became life-minded only after learning hard lessons through illnesses and deaths in my family, and from tough feedback, and from watching others get it right.

The concept of high performance is usually discussed in one of two aspects, in sports and at work. High performers in sports operate at an elite level, physically and mentally, as individuals and as teammates. They leverage coaches, sponsors, and their own drive to improve every day. They need playing time to stay relevant and confident. High performers at work are similar in many ways. They push beyond their literal job description. They self-initiate. They excel across the work, the people, and the politics. They are trusted with special projects, embrace stretch assignments, and often enjoy accelerated promotions. They exhibit epic levels of resilience, perseverance, and resourcefulness. They often engage coaches, sponsors, and mentors to build their clarity and confidence.

Interestingly, some of the highest performers at work also show the highest anxiety during times of organizational change, such as mergers, downturns, or major leadership shifts. They can be some of the first to flee during times of uncertainty because high performers need to feel both valued and in control.[2] Like the elite athlete's need for playing time, high performers at work need to see a career path and have a high degree of confidence that it's paved for them.

Beyond sports and work, a third aspect of high performance exists, whole-person high performance. My promotion to partner was a moment to celebrate as a high performer, but my corresponding prediabetic HbA1c levels were not. My client's big bonus was such a proud high-performer moment, but he was alone at forty and didn't

[2] Robin Abrahams, Boris Groysberg, and Steven L. Manchel, "The COVID-19 Mutiny," *Working Knowledge*, June 22, 2021.

want to be. A mentor allowed her passion for music to evaporate like a jet stream as she achieved million-miler flyer status. Cultivating the role you want work to play in your life is required for true high performance, whole-person high performance.

> You have to put work to work for you.

Let's do the math for the typical high performer at work. Assuming you sleep seven hours each night, in a seven-day period, you're awake and working or preparing in some way for work more hours than you're awake doing absolutely nothing related to work. The math alone shows just how important it is that work be in service of the life you want to live. You have to put work to work for you. This requires knowing what gets a yes and what gets a no. In other words, you need a strategy.

In business, the best definition of having a strategy is knowing what to say no to. In life, it's no different. Have a strategy for the life you want to live and the role work will play in that life. The more you *know* what you want, the better you are at saying *no* to the clutter that distorts your path. Knowing means no-ing. When you know your core values, you make quality decisions. When you know your priorities, you filter the day-to-day distractions. When you know your strengths and interests, you stay fresh and relevant for the future you want to have.

To put work in its desired place, you must have options. When you have options, you are in control. Neuroscience shows how surrounding ourselves with options allows us to move more calmly and flexibly through life's changes (intentional reactivity) and to shape the future we want to live in with intentional proactivity.[3] This book provides strategies for surrounding yourself with options so you're always making decisions from a position of strength.

---

[3] Sheena S. Iyengar, Lauren A. Leotti, Kevin N. Oschner, "Born to Choose: The Origins and Value of Need for Control," *Trends in Cognitive Sciences* 14, 10 (October 2010): 457-63.

From the hundreds of people I've interviewed and thousands I've coached, I have mapped the career journeys of high performers. These journeys vary in pattern, sequence, and velocity, but each high performer traverses three moments that matter throughout their career.

I have given each of these three career moments a persona:

- Exploration Erika: "I want more."
- Crossroads K.T.: "I must now decide."
- Hamster-Wheel Hank: "I'm stuck."

I was Crossroads K.T. at age thirty, pursuing an MBA to make a significant career switch from acting to business. I was Hamster-Wheel Hank at forty, when I let work erode my health and relationships. I was Exploration Erika at fifty, when I returned to school, re-tired (as in got new tires), and launched The Me-Suite.

Where are you in this moment? Since you're reading this book (and thank you), you identify as a high performer. You strive to have a meaningful career. You're good at what you do. You take pride in what you accomplish. You have high standards for yourself and those around you. People admire your strengths. You want that next promotion, the new title, the big raise, the top-tier performance rating, the increased accountability, the new experiences. You enjoy the rush and the rewards. You like to learn and grow. You want to make a difference. You are principled and interesting and complex.

Yes, and you sometimes think, "What if I changed companies?" or "Is now the time to start that business?" or "Do I want to keep doing this type of work?" Your health may not always be where you want it to be. You need to call that friend you've been meaning to call. Your relationship may need a recharge. COVID, the economy, or other external factors might have caused you to think, proactively or reactively, "I'm not sure exactly what I want, but I know it isn't this."

You may be in a groove of sorts, but more from routine inertia than from evolutionary energy. You may be hungry for the next big challenge.

Perhaps you are:

- a career professional at a crossroads
- a next-generation leader at a nexus
- a manager who wants more
- an executive considering an exit

At your core, you're a high-performing professional. You know your career, however you define it, plays a significant role in your life. No apologies for that. Sometimes that looks like being on the road a good bit. Other times it shows up as working a few hours after dinner or checking your emails before you get out of bed. Although others might see this as working too much, you are unapologetic about your drive and your focus on career because you value that part of yourself and the difference you make. This isn't about work-life balance. It's about work being in service to your vision of your future. This doesn't just happen; you have to cultivate it. The options you cultivate are results of your intentional, thoughtful actions. Like a landscape architect, you're planting for the future, for both shade and sun, for rain and drought, for heat and cold, annuals and perennials, taking control of what each season offers.

You've picked up the right book as a career-driven, life-minded professional who wants control of your future, who is deliberate and planful about the role work plays in supporting the life you want to live.

Whether you're Exploration Erika, Crossroads K.T., or Hamster-Wheel Hank, options are power. Let's get in there.

OPTIONS ARE POWER

Clocks had just turned back an hour for fall, so the parking lot was dark when I left the office that cool Monday evening. When I approached my car, the sound of someone puking startled me. Anyone who's eaten street food from a stall with no electricity, despite all your friends and guidebooks telling you not to do so, knows that sound. I walked cautiously toward the BMW a few spots down and found my buddy Marco. He was bent over with one hand on his knee and the other holding his computer bag out to the side to save it from the spray.

"Marco, are you okay?" I asked while reaching to help with the bag.

"I don't know what I'm gonna do."

"What happened? Do you need a doctor?" I asked.

"No, no, nothing like that. They just let me go. I'm out of a job. What am I gonna do?"

Marco straightened, looked up at the sky, and covered his face with his hands. The shock had his mind spinning for a few minutes. He rambled. "That big, new house, the kids' private school. We'll have to cancel the vacation. Jan will have to go back to work. I haven't interviewed in forever." Marco felt trapped. And these were only the financial traps that first flooded his worried mind.

Feeling trapped also manifests in non-financial ways, such as when you're bored, demotivated, unfulfilled, unsupported, frustrated, ill, or just feel stuck. You know *intuitively* that not feeling trapped is a good thing. You feel empowered when you have choices, selections, options. You also know *biologically* that not feeling trapped is a good thing. Neuroscience[4] shows humans have a natural reaction in the amygdala region of the brain when we feel threatened or trapped. The amygdala was designed to protect us from danger. Indeed, it's the part of the brain being referenced with the phrase "fight or flight response." The overwhelming anxiety you

[4] Arlin Cuncic, "Ámygdala Hijack and The Fight or Flight Response," *Very Well Mind*, June 22, 2021, https://www.verywellmind.com/what-happens-during-an-amygdala-hijack-4165944.

can feel when trapped in a personal or professional situation is likely an amygdala response giving you the sense that you've lost control.

In contrast, perceiving you have options gives you a calming sense of being in control and the power to choose your next best move. Certainly, there is so much you cannot control about your circumstances and life events, so focus on getting power and flexibility and resilience by controlling what you can.

> Options give you the *right,* not the *obligation*, to make a change.

"Options are power" is my mantra. Although, I don't yet have any ink, when this book sells a thousand copies, I commit to getting a tattoo that says: "Options are power." You can hold me to that promise. "Options are power" is at the heart of my approach to brain-based executive coaching. Options give high-performing leaders the *right*, not the *obligation*, to make a change. Simply put, options put you in control. My life mission is to help career-driven, life-minded individuals surround themselves with options to shape the future they want to live in. And the irony isn't lost on me that I want to promote options by putting permanent ink on my body. That shows how strongly I believe in the power of options. I don't plan to change my mind on this one.

Humans have a psychological and biological need to be in control. When we feel in control, our brain's frontal lobes enable rational decision-making and controlled responses. We recognize, understand, and manage our emotions with calm. Behavioral studies [5] and neuroimaging work across pigeons, monkeys, rats, and humans show signs of stress reduction and a higher sense of reward and motivation when we have options because we are in control.

[5] Sheena S. Iyengar, Lauren A. Leotti, Kevin N. Oschner, "Born to Choose: The Origins and Value of Need for Control," *Trends in Cognitive Sciences* 14, 10 (October 2010): 457-63.

When we feel the opposite of in control—trapped, threatened, cornered—the brain's frontal lobes shut down, and the amygdala takes over in what psychologist Daniel Goleman[6] calls "amygdala hijack." Stress hormones, including cortisol and adrenaline, are released. The body may then overreact to stress by experiencing a rapid heartbeat, sweating, increased blood sugar, or agitation. During amygdala hijack, the mind and body are in a state that is the opposite of calm.

The science shows how surrounding ourselves with options allows us to move more calmly and flexibly through life's changes (intentional reactivity) and to shape the future we want to live in (intentional proactivity).

The Me-Suite ontology nurtures your universe of options by building discipline in these seven areas:

1. Core Values: non-negotiables you expect of yourself and others
2. Primacy: the most important thing to get right at this moment
3. Personal Brand: what people think and feel when they hear your name
4. Relationships: keeping your network deposits and withdrawals in balance
5. Skills and Strengths: thinking creatively and broadly about the value you bring
6. Physical and Mental Health: controlling the controllables
7. Finances: making informed, planful decisions about money

[6] Kimberly Holland, "Amygdala Hijack: When Emotion Takes Over," *Healthline*, September 17, 2021, https://www.healthline.com/health/stress/amygdala-hijack.

Core Values: Non-negotiables You Expect of Yourself and Others

In December 2019, I met a CEO just before the COVID-19 pandemic lockdown. He's an intense personality. The kind of leader who looks you in the eye. Really. We were beginning a collaboration, getting to know each other's businesses. I started by asking about his company's goals for 2020, his core services, his target customers—the usual MBA type of buzzwordy questions.

"What would be helpful for me to share with you about The Me-Suite?" I asked.

My new CEO friend replied with a sincere, neutral expression, "Who *are* you?"

I paused a beat. *He really means that the way it sounded. He wants to know who I am.* He wasn't asking the core values of The Me-Suite. He was asking the core values of Donna Peters as a person. Of course, I was not only ready to share, having given such a question so much thought in recent years, but I also found a kindred leadership spirit that day. And doesn't his question make perfect sense? Companies and organizations are made up of people. The people—not the posters, annual reports, and org charts—possess core values.

> Core values are the non-negotiable rudder steering the key decisions you make.

Core values are not a wish list of how you aspire to behave. They are how you behave right now. Core values represent not only how you want to show up in the world, but also what you expect from others. Think about a company you most admire. Check out the core values on their website. Core values steer the way the company and its C-suite team satisfy a need, operate with purpose, and create value for the long term. Those core values are not just on posters yellowing in the hallways. They are foundational to hiring and training; they inform performance evaluations; they guide decisions that impact the future. When they're violated, they get people in big trouble and make headline news.

The greatest responsibility of a C-suite leadership team is to define and marshal the core values of the company. The companies you most admire have core values front and center of all key decisions, of all rewards and punishments. Perhaps the most iconic example of a company living its core values is Johnson & Johnson and its company credo. In 1982, seven consumers died after ingesting cyanide-laced capsules of Extra-Strength TYLENOL. The company recalled thirty-one million bottles from store shelves, quickly replacing the bottles with tamper-proof packaging. This response sparked an industry norm and created one of the most admirable public relations stories in our lifetime, still taught in business schools and ethics classes to this day.[7] I know the power of the credo firsthand. On my first day as a Johnson & Johnson employee in 1996, I received a framed copy of Our Credo for my desk. I attended training on Our Credo and heard colleagues reference Our Credo almost daily. It was then, and is now, in the DNA of the organization.

A more recent example of a company living its core values is Patagonia. In October 2021, CEO Ryan Gellert, boycotted all Facebook advertising and encouraged other businesses to do the

[7] Judith Rehak, "Tylenol Made a Hero of Johnson & Johnson: The Recall That Started Them All," *The International Harold Tribune*, March 23, 2002, https://www.nytimes.com/2002/03/23/your-money/IHT-tylenol-made-a-hero-of-johnson-johnson-the-recall-that-started.html.

same.[8] He believed the Facebook (now Meta) platform was allowing hate speech and misinformation about climate change in violation of two of Patagonia's core values: 1) Cause no unnecessary harm, and 2) Use business to protect nature.[9]

To begin or refresh your personal core values, start by studying the core values of companies you admire. How do these companies behave when you are looking? And when you are not looking? Take Starbucks, for example.

Starbucks's core values[10] are:

- Creating a culture of warmth and belonging, where everyone is welcome.
- Delivering our very best in all we do, holding ourselves accountable for results.
- Acting with courage, challenging the status quo, and finding new ways to grow our company and each other.
- Being present, connecting with transparency, dignity, and respect.

The first core value was violated in 2018 when a White barista called police on Black men in a Philadelphia store. "The company's founding values are based on humanity and inclusion," said Executive Chairman Howard Schultz. "We will learn from our mistakes and reaffirm our commitment to creating a safe and welcoming environment for every customer." [11] Because of the

---

[8] Matt Egan, Patagonia CEO: Companies Should Join Us in Boycotting Facebook, https://www.cnn.com/2021/10/28/business/patagonia-ceo-facebook-boycott/index.html, October 28, 2021.

[9] Patagonia, https://www.patagonia.com/core-values/, November 11, 2021.

[10] "Our Values," Starbucks, October 3, 2021, https://www.starbucks.com/careers/working-at-starbucks/culture-and-values.

[11] "Starbucks to Close All Stores Nationwide for Racial-Bias Education May 29," Starbucks, April 17, 2018, https://stories.starbucks.com/press/2018/starbucks-to-close-stores-nationwide-for-racial-bias-education-may-29/.

incident and violation of Starbucks's core values, 8,000 stores closed to provide racial-bias training to 175,000 employees.

Simone Biles[12] showed alignment with her core values when she made the significant move from Nike to Athleta. Athleta's core values[13] are: Women for Women, Inclusive Community, and People & Planet.

Consistently living its core values propelled Virgin Atlantic[14] to an excellent Net Promoter Score of 51 in 2021[15]. These core values also receive an A+ from me for simplicity, memorability, and ability to induce a smile: Think red. Make friends. Be amazing.

Alibaba's core values[16] have been a source of inspiration for many. They are written as provocative statements about expected behaviors and mindsets.

Alibaba's core values are:

- Customers first, employees second, shareholders third.
- Trust makes everything simple.
- Change is the only constant.
- Today's best performance is tomorrow's baseline.
- If not now, when? If not me, who?
- Live seriously, work happily.

Yet, these core values fell short in 2021 when the company faced allegations of female harassment and assault after years of public

---

[12] Kevin Draper, "Simone Biles Leaves Nike for Sponsor That Focuses on Women," *New York Times,* April 23, 2021, updated August 7, 2021, https://www.nytimes.com/2021/04/23/sports/olympics/simone-biles-athleta-nike.html.

[13] "Our Values," Athleta, October 3, 2021, https://athleta.gap.com/browse/info.do?cid=1074427.

[14] "The Virgin Atlantic Mission Statement," Virgin Atlantic, October 3, 2021, https://mission-statement.com/virgin-atlantic/.

[15] "Virgin Atlantic Net Promoter Score 2021 Benchmark," Customer Guru, October 3, 2021, https://netpromoterscore.guru/virgin-atlantic-com.

[16] "Culture and Values," Alibaba Group, October 3, 2021, https://www.alibabagroup.com/en/about/culture.

support of women's equality.[17] Alibaba subsequently committed to creating a Committee on Workplace Environment, reporting to the board, to realign its core values.[18] Its changes had a noticeable impact on the global business community, particularly its competitor, Amazon. After pressure and reflection on social justice issues, particularly sustainability and inclusion, Jeff Bezos, CEO of Amazon, added two leadership principles in 2021: 1) Strive to be the Earth's best employer, and 2) Success and scale bring broad responsibility.[19]

Airbnb championed their core values in 2021 when they offered free housing to 20,000 Afghan refugees.[20] "We're united with our community to create a world where anyone can belong anywhere."[21]

Just like the companies and organizations you most admire, you exist to satisfy a need, to operate with purpose, to create value. You are surely in it for the long term, and it's likely time to articulate your own core values in a deliberate, thoughtful way, to formally share them with those people most important to you, and to revisit them with regularity to see how well the decisions you make are lining up

---

[17] Sui-Lee Wee, Raymon Zhong, "After Proudly Celebrating Women, Alibaba Faces Reckoning Over Harassment," *The New York Times,* September 1, 2021, updated September 7, 2021, https://www.nytimes.com/2021/09/01/technology/china-alibaba-rape-metoo.html.

[18] Shen Lu, "Alibaba Details New Sexual Misconduct Policies," Protocol, August 12, 2021, https://www.protocol.com/bulletins/alibaba-sexual-harassment-policy-details.

[19] Luciana Paulise, "Jeff Bezos Adds 2 Leadership Principles Before Retiring as Amazon's CEO," *Forbes*, July 2, 2021, https://www.forbes.com/sites/lucianapaulise/2021/07/02/jeff-bezos-adds-2-leadership-principles-before-retiring-as-amazons-ceo/?sh=28be13cc723a.

[20] "The Airbnb Community's Support of Afghan Refugees," Airbnb, August 24, 2021, https://news.airbnb.com/afghan-refugees/.

[21] Lattice Team, "How Defining Values and Culture Helped Airbnb Achieve Worldwide Success," October 3 2017, https://lattice.com/library/how-defining-values-and-culture-helped-airbnb-achie.

to those values. Similar to those admired companies, lead your life with the foundation of core values.

Start by asking:

- What are my core values?
- What are examples of how I make decisions aligned with my core values?
- Are there examples when I make decisions against my core values?
- If I'm straying from my core values, how do I come back to center?

Since core values are so fundamental to who we are, all guests on *The Me-Suite* podcast are first asked to share their core values and how those values drive key decisions in their lives. Across hundreds of interviews, core values cluster in the following top themes.

Other guests use phrases, such as:

- Failure isn't fatal unless you don't learn from it.
- Pay it forward/Give back.
- Show up/Be present.
- Do everything with pride and commitment.
- Get out of your comfort zone.
- Make others feel special.
- Solve for the greater good.
- Motivate and be motivated.
- Don't take yourself too seriously.
- If it's not a h*ll yes, it's a no.

As inspiration in creating your own core values, start with examples from the companies you most admire, a similar exercise to what I shared above. Then, think about where you prioritize your time and how you make key decisions. Think about the people you choose to bring into or leave out of your life. Perhaps think about a time when you stepped away from what was right for you. How did that feel? These experiences are good indicators of your inherent core values.

At a time in my career when I was showered with accelerated promotions, I was feeling pretty mighty (a nice word for arrogant). When I had a new client with a challenge I had seen before, I thought, *I've got this. I've been to this rodeo before.* I jumped impatiently to a solution rather than listening first, and the client felt ignored and disrespected. My core values are curiosity, freedom, and respect. By violating the first and third, I didn't serve the client in the way they needed, and I was removed from the project.

My core values are curiosity, freedom, and respect. I came to understand these after personal reflection and testing the list with trusted loved ones and colleagues.

Curiosity. I love to learn new topics. I am interested in each person. I believe this was one driver of my career in the theatre. As a professional actor, I made a living putting myself in other people's shoes, understanding a situation from another's point of view. I want to understand why people think and feel as they do. What motivates them. Why we may agree or disagree. I like to learn and explore, to connect the dots. Curiosity has driven me to school many times.

I majored in English and have an MBA from Cornell with Distinction, an MFA from UNC-Chapel Hill, and an executive coaching diploma from Emory University. Curiosity has also propelled me through careers that appear to be tangents to some. In addition to acting professionally, I've owned a restaurant, taught English in South Korea, retired as a senior partner after twenty years in management consulting, and now am an executive coach and award-winning podcast host. As an executive coach, I listen to learn who the person is. I help them balance aspirations with practicality.

Freedom. Perhaps fueled by the curiosity mentioned above, I've always wanted to have the freedom to change my mind, to not be painted into a corner, and I want others to feel the same. For me, this comes from living below my means, financially, and allowing relationships into my life that nurture my sense that everything is possible. Freedom allows me to be fully invested in the decisions I make because I make them willingly and revocably—with agency. As a career coach, I help high performers see the possible and challenge their limiting beliefs.

Respect. We each deserve equality, fairness, and civility. In the words of my great-uncle, Carl Elliott Sr., first-ever recipient of the John F. Kennedy Profile in Courage Award, "Early in my life, I became aware that brains and ability knew no economic, racial, or other distinction."[22] As a life coach, I respect the individual and all we have to learn from each other.

Given that no one can go through the pandemic unchanged, and inspired by others in The Me-Suite community, I am contemplating the addition of two core values: gratitude and vitality.

---

[22] "Carl Elliott, Sr," John F. Kennedy Presidential Library and Museum, October 3, 2021, https://www.jfklibrary.org/events-and-awards/profile-in-courage-award/award-recipients/carl-elliott-sr-1990.

Identifying your personal core values is a meaningful exercise to conduct alone for self-reflection and an energizing exercise to conduct with life partners, closest friends, children, colleagues, and mentors. A listener of *The Me-Suite* podcast shared that he and his wife had a core values conversation during COVID. He was in the U.S. with their five-year-old daughter. The wife was grounded in South Korea, unable to travel. Over video, they talked about their core values and aligned as a couple in the way they wanted to lead their family. The daughter shared her core values too: "Mind my teacher" and "Love my momma."

A client insightfully recognized that her core values—family and personal growth—were sometimes in conflict with one another. While her extended family relied on her for financial and emotional support, she wanted to take on a significant career relocation opportunity. She resolved the tension through open dialogue and alignment of expectations with loved ones and work mentors.

Show me how you spend your time, what you reward and reject, and I'll show you your core values. Consider using colored sticky notes to capture initial words and phrases that come to mind as you reflect on your values. To narrow the list to its essence, eliminate overlaps and synonyms. Eliminate attributes you only wish you exhibited but put zero time toward. Core values represent who you are in your soul, not how you wish to be some day. Strive to land three to five core values. A targeted, manageable list helps you synthesize duplicate concepts and increase memorability. Have you ever worked at a company with a long core values list? You can usually recite about four of them, and anything after that is a struggle to remember. Your core values should be so clear to you that you can recite them as innately as your birth date.

Another tool for helping to identify your personal core values is to think about the opposite. Think about companies you've stopped supporting because they do not represent what you value. Think about individuals you don't trust or respect because of some behavior they exhibit that you find offensive. Thinking about what you're repelled by is powerful inspiration for landing your personal core values. In season 1 of *The Me-Suite* podcast, CEOs Shawn Walker and Ana Dutra talk about how they thought about the opposite—what repels them—to derive their personal core values.

I'm often asked, "Do core values change over time?" As a former management consultant, I am trained to recognize that there is rarely a single, right answer, so I have to start with "It depends." Across my hundreds of interviews on this topic, I've observed three approaches.

The first and most common approach is to have a foundational list of three to five core values. Whether you are Exploration Erika, Crossroads K.T., or Hamster-Wheel Hank, your core values are a personal compass helping you make the next big decisions. They represent the constant you across all stages of your life. In my interviews, the number of core values ranges from one to seven, with three being the most common number. Three seems to be the magic number of core values that we can hold in our heads, easily share with others, and put into practice.

With the second approach, many people add one or two values as significant changes occur in their lives, often sparked by health and/or family events. Additional values such as balance, authenticity, and being present begin to emerge. Just as with corporate boards, timely issues around social justice and sustainability are also fueling a fresh look at individual core values and the impact our decisions have on others. One client recently added "Leave everything better than I found it." Another added "equality."

The third approach is to revisit core values annually, often finessing the wording to get the intention just right. For example, one client started with a core value of health and later evolved it to vitality. Another client began with relationships and evolved the value to connection.

Identifying your core values and putting them at the center of your decisions, as admired C-suites do, will help you know what to accept and what to reject. You will have filters and guideposts for making the best decisions and the most significant changes, for choosing the best options, whenever they present themselves. That's a powerful feeling. Do the work to identify your core values and check in on them at least annually. How about each year during the month of your birthday? If you need some time to roll around in this topic for a bit, to get to the essence of those core values that fit you just right, consider the words and phrases from The Me-Suite community as inspiration.

Example Core Values from The Me-Suite Community

Accountability	**Authenticity**	**Carpe Diem**
commitment	be you	be present
responsibility	transparency	each day counts
pride	courage	life is short
Connection	**Determination**	**Empathy**
loyalty	effort matters	equality
community	grit	justice
team first	perseverance	humility
Energy	**Growth**	**Integrity**
creativity	curiosity	honesty
positivity	adventure	trust
gratitude	adaptability	candor
Purpose	**Stewardship**	**Well-being**
vision	inspire	vitality
passion	give back	self-care
impact	helpfulness	wellness

Hear *The Me-Suite* podcast guests share their core values at the top of every episode, on all podcast apps and at www.the-me-suite.com/podcast. Also, check out www.the-me-suite.com/tools for more quick tips to create or refine your own personal core values.

Primacy: The Most Important Thing to Get Right at This Moment

In my coaching practice, I hear very well-intentioned, intelligent people struggling to articulate what they really want. I often hear: "It's not about the money," and then we spend a whole session on negotiating a higher salary." I hear: "I'm willing to relocate for the right opportunity," and then the person realizes moving isn't an option for their spouse. The more common disconnect is when they say, "I want to be doing something more challenging," and then they realize the extra work of changing companies or starting a new business isn't what they want to sign up for right now. These discrepancies are not character flaws. They are simply examples of the thoughtful work that must be done to be honest with yourself about what you really want and need right now, in this moment. Power comes from being clear about what you really want right now and having options available to help you get it.

The Power of Primacy Pathing

High-performing professionals identify their goals and forge a path to achieve them. On one hand, this may seem obvious. Like, duh, of course high performers have goals and achieve them. They're high performing. On the other hand, high performers want to conquer the next achievement. They often are a bit restless, have many interests and champions and high standards, making it difficult to prioritize a path. What others admire about high performers is their pursuit of the next best move. What can be a real challenge for high performers is prioritizing what matters most in that moment.

There is no such thing as a perfect situation, and primacy pathing helps prioritize the most important thing to get right, right now. High performers have a lot of plates spinning. The truth is not everything can be a priority. You can't work on everything at once, and indeed, not everything is of equal importance all the time. Some things in your life may be moving smoothly enough, while others need attention. The important things here are self-awareness and intention.

Let's look at an example of how an Exploration Erika might approach primacy. Exploration Erika says, "I want more." She finds great clarity in a primacy exercise. A client in the lane of Exploration Erika had a terrific run in large corporations and was hungry for a senior leadership position. This Erika wanted more—a true C-suite position, to have the full accountability of running a company, an actual P&L. A C-suite opportunity came to Erika fairly quickly at a smaller organization, which was no surprise.

A C-suite role at a smaller organization was the likely next best move to put a C-suite title at a Fortune 500 company on her resume in the next one to two years. At the same time, Erika was a bit deflated by the compensation of the C-suite offer. The offer was about fifteen percent better than her current salary, but she had thought the senior title would come with a more significant increase. This troubled Erika. She wanted the title *and* expected significantly more compensation for that title.

Through coaching, Erika discovered she hadn't really settled into her primacy. Did she care more about maximizing title or maximizing total compensation at this moment? After self-reflection and analyzing her motivations, Erika chose title. With compensation roughly on par with her current corporate role, she moved to a C-suite position with the smaller company. Her primacy, at that moment, was to maximize her leadership accountability experience to build her longer-term board story, even if her compensation only slightly improved with this move.

In this example, Erika realized what really mattered most at this moment was the title and personal growth. It was hard for her to admit this at first. Pursuing a title alone felt hierarchical and shallow to her.

We worked through that self-limiting belief to reframe what it would mean to build a resume of CXO titles and growth experiences—to build experiences that propped her up for the paid board options she wanted to surround herself with later in her career. We also worked through realistic, fact-based salary expectations for this type of role at this size company in this industry.

I saw myself in Exploration Erika. Out of graduate school, I wanted to work internationally and asked anyone who'd listen to assign me outside the United States. International career experience had primacy for me. A few months later, I had an offer to work in Switzerland for one year on a merger. This sounded so perfect, until I was told the merger work would be change management. I didn't want to do that type of "squishy" work and honestly didn't respect it that much.

I consulted a mentor. She helped me realize that international work experience had primacy for me at that moment. She also called me out on my self-limiting belief, encouraging me to *embrace* the change-management experience I'd gain, not *judge* it. So off I went to Switzerland for a year. I gained the international experience I craved, working on a merger across five countries. And ironically, I gained tremendous admiration for the change-management discipline, becoming the lead of a significant change-management practice later in my career.

Crossroads K.T. is the one who must now decide, and finds relief in a primacy exercise. Primacy helps Crossroads K.T. run *to* something, not *from* something. This is an important mindset since Crossroads K.T. most often is experiencing a deficit—perhaps a personal relationship isn't getting the attention it needs. Perhaps K.T.'s health is not where he wants it to be. Maybe a passion or hobby is atrophying. Maybe a core value is being tested. A primacy exercise helps Crossroads K.T. shine a light on what he most wants to get right. If the answer is "more time with family," K.T. learns better delegation at work or avoids work emails on Saturdays. If the answer is "get back in shape," K.T.

hires a trainer or gets a workout buddy. If the answer is "save for retirement," K.T. surrounds himself with expert advice and calls a family meeting.

I was Crossroads K.T. when I was spending five days a week away from home and working on weekends. My husband needled me one weekend at the lake as I worked at the dining room table. "Are you saving lives or stamping out disease?" he asked. I chuckled. "Neither," I said, as I somewhat reluctantly put my computer away. We went fishing for the rest of the afternoon, and it was glorious. At a minimum, my relationship deserved to have primacy on the weekends, didn't it? The truth is I was so busy looking busy with my own self-imposed extra projects and artificial urgency that I was ignoring my self-defined core values.

I began watching how others in my organization pushed back on deadlines. I learned how they negotiated for more time on non-critical matters. It was important to me that I looked eager and all-in even while I was pushing back, so I practiced a few approaches until I found the one that worked for me. If someone asked for something "by Monday," for example, I'd start by saying, "I have commitments this weekend. Would Tuesday be all right for this?" The one time I recall my request being denied was when my boss asked if I could get it done over the weekend if he got another person to help me. It wasn't perfect, but it was a starting place.

Hamster-Wheel Hank, the one who feels stuck, finds great energy in primacy. A Hamster-Wheel Hank approached me at the start of the pandemic. He did something really well, and then people wanted him to keep doing that one thing. Because he was so good at it and he had a great attitude while doing it, people assumed he must really enjoy it. This happens to a lot of high performers, but often, the opposite is true.

You were good at the activity, and happy to do it once to help out, but now that you're being put in a box doing this same thing over and over, you're B-O-R-E-D. You've become branded, known for something that isn't the brand you want to have. A primacy exercise helps Hamster-Wheel Hank imagine the short term and ask, "Will I be proud if I'm doing this same thing six months from now?"

One Hank I coached decided to apply for a transfer within the same company, a great move that balanced his risk-aversion (stay in the same company) with his primacy for adventure (new industry area). Interestingly, another Hank completed the primacy exercise and decided she wanted to stay on the hamster wheel for now. She realized the hamster wheel gave her great autonomy to flex her schedule around her kids and provided some free time to develop a side business she wanted to launch. The primacy exercise helped her reframe her mindset about the repetitive, stale role. She realized the ease of that role fueled her ability to grow a separate path. In a sense, she was Hamster-Wheel Hank and Exploration Erika at the same time.

You may also see yourself as Hamster-Wheel Hank if a promotion or other role advancement isn't coming as quickly as you expected. Maybe the career path seems ill-defined or too long and winding. In this case, looking externally—job interviewing—can be a terrific way to test your value in the market. See what's out there, and if you decide to stay, you'll do so from an informed position, rather than from a position of inertia.

I was Hamster-Wheel Hank when I had become the go-to program lead for complex, global-transformation programs. People assumed that since I excelled at execution with my organization and conflict-resolution skills, I must enjoy doing that all the time. And they were right to think so because I hadn't given anyone a reason to think differently. I moved from one project to the next, doing that thing I do and going where the business needed me. When Sunday nights began to induce a groan, I knew something had to change.

Most aspects of my life were running smoothly at that point. It was time for personal growth to take primacy. I wanted to move into business development to flex my creativity muscles. I knew I had a lot to offer if I could reignite my theatre background in some way in this corporate environment. Sales pitches and workshop facilitation seemed like a great combination.

I worked with a coach to refine my ask and get energized to leverage my network. I began telling the narrative I needed people to hear about my desired next moves. They often told me, "I had no idea that wasn't the work you wanted to do. I thought you really enjoyed it since you are so good at it." It took about eighteen months to move fully into the work I wanted to be doing at that stage, and it took mobilizing my network of supporters to achieve it.

> What has primacy for you at this moment in your life?

When you're seeking the next best step for yourself, answer this single question: "What has primacy for me at this moment in my life?" The question is simple. The answer can be quite hard to land. For example, when it comes to work and career, there is no perfect role. Perfect roles do not exist. What does exist is a role that serves your most important needs at this moment. You just have to define for yourself what that is. That's the hard part because it requires self-reflection and decisiveness. Three tools are powerful in shining a light on what has primacy—the one thing you must get right at this moment. The answer is different for everyone. The answer changes over time. Embrace these three primacy tools as your life and relationships evolve.

Download The Me-Suite Primacy Pathing Tool at www.the-me-suite.com/tools.

A Tribute to Working Parents Everywhere

Primacy Pathing is particularly challenging for my clients who are parents of young children. These clients have made me reflect on my own behavior as a child of dual-career parents. Here, I apologize for the times my brother and I imposed nuclear levels of stress on my full-time working parents.

- When I was just learning to talk, I called the daycare lady "Momma." After that, Mom moved to night shift for a while.
- At almost three years old, I ate a whole bottle of chewable baby aspirin since I loved the taste of Sweet Tarts. Dad took me to the hospital where Mom was working the night shift in the children's unit. They made me vomit, and we went home.
- That time I cried and cried because I didn't want to go to daycare. I was the oldest kid there, and the lady made me babysit the other kids. I cleverly bargained with Dad to get a little plastic swimming pool.
- When I was about nine years old, I hung out on the side of a busy highway alone for a few hours. Mom and Dad got their wires crossed and each thought the other one was picking me up from school after work.
- That time Mom ran in to grab the phone and my toddler brother took off walking in the backyard woods with the Dalmatian, Dolly (named after Parton). Helicopter searches and hours later, my brother was found safe and exhausted.
- Around age ten or so, I wasn't prepared for a test and wanted to take a sick day. I mixed talcum powder, water, and orange food coloring to make "throw up" and put it on the carpet by my bed. Not only was I in trouble for lying, but Mom also had permanently stained carpet and was late to work.
- At thirteen, I was home alone in the summer, and a felon, fresh out on parole, broke into the house. Ironically, I was watching *One Life to Live*. The cops later said, "Donna was calm. Her parents were incoherent."

Happily, the only stress I've caused my parents in my adult years has been from eloping and keeping my last name.

Primacy Pathing Tool #1: What Matters Most

Do a Google search on the topic of work and life. My search yielded almost two billion resources and more than one hundred thousand books. On the topic of the 2021 Great Resignation alone, almost 250 million results appeared. Clearly, the interplay of work and life doesn't rest. So many thoughtful researchers, coaches, therapists, and real people with real experiences have written on having it all, juggling it all, making sense of it all.

As an executive coach certified in the neuroscience of leadership, I've reviewed much of the work in this field, including Tom and Zig Ziglar's Wheel of Life[23], Tony Robbins's Pyramid of Mastery[24], James Clear's *Atomic Habits,* the podcast insights of Brené Brown's *Unlocking Us* and Adam Grant's *WorkLife,* and the work of prolific research authors Dr. Suzy Green, Dr. Rick Gilkey, Dr. David Rock, and Dr. Jeffrey Schwartz. Of course, so many others exist, and I don't intend to insult them with my omissions. The scholars' research and my experience coaching thousands of high performers informed my approach to identifying what matters most to you right now, at this moment. I call this Primacy Pathing, looking your priorities in the face and identifying your options for going after those priorities.

Primacy Pathing requires reflecting on these seven dimensions:

1. Career: your strengths, your ambitions, your path
2. Finances: your money now and forever, your decisions, your behavior

[23] Tom Ziglar, "The Wheel of Life," Ziglar, October 3, 2021, https://www.ziglar.com/articles/the-wheel-of-life/.
[24] Tony Robbins, "Tie It All Together," Tony Robbins, October 3, 2021, https://www.tonyrobbins.com/leadership-impact/tie-it-all-together/.

3. Family: your expectations, your commitments, your needs
4. Health: your physical and mental vitality
5. Personal Growth: your evolution
6. Spirituality: your mindfulness, your calm, your purpose
7. Relationships: your connections, your give-and-take

To create your Primacy Path, place a circle on the spectrum to indicate your satisfaction with each dimension in your life today. Place a star where you want that dimension to be in the next year. It is completely acceptable to say you are fine where you are, on track, no change required. In fact, I love it when clients have clarity on what to say no to. In this exercise, we're looking for the satisfaction gaps that have urgency. Your primacy—what is most important to you at this moment in time—is likely where the largest satisfaction gap resides.

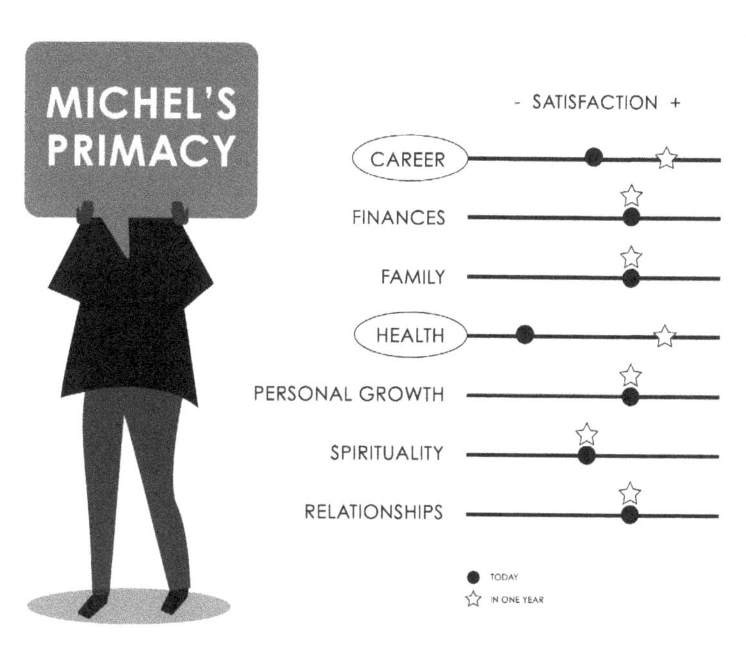

The example diagram shown here is from a client. Michel had the largest satisfaction gap on the health dimension, with career coming in a clear second. It may come as no surprise, and be all too familiar, that the pressure of climbing the career ladder helped Michel gain twenty pounds over a few years. When Michel first began working with me, the goal was to "seek a less demanding job." After reflection on the primacy exercise, Michel's goal became instead to "make time for my health." The biggest move Michel made was talking with the global team to align on conference call times.

Previously, Michel had hosted conference calls beginning at 7:00 a.m. Eastern time to accommodate the various global time zones. The team came together to agree on rotating call times throughout the week. They also decided to cancel one of the standing calls altogether. Voilà! Because of the primacy exercise, three days suddenly opened up as opportunities for Michel to sleep a little longer, or exercise, or grab a healthful breakfast, or meditate during the week. Prior to the primacy exercise, Michel thought a whole, complex job search was required. After the primacy exercise, the smallest step was the only one needed to fill the most significant gap at that moment.

A more complicated example involved a client in a dual-career relationship. Andrea's primacy at the time was career acceleration. She felt her career was stalling a bit. She wanted a senior title and higher pay. However, she couldn't relocate, given her partner's career.

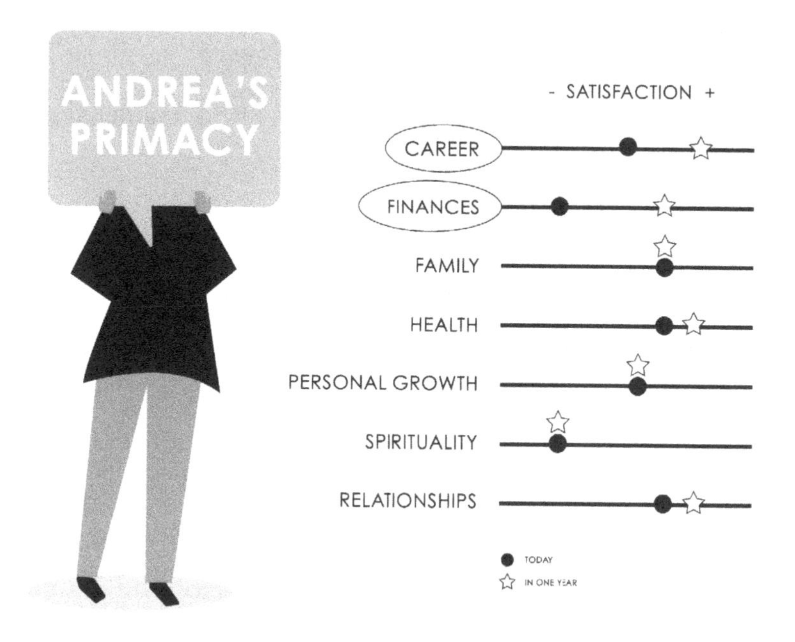

In this primacy example, finances showed the most significant gap, with career coming in a close second. Fast forward, and Andrea launched a job search over several months, landing two attractive offers. One offer was a senior title at a smaller company with compensation in line with her expectations of a fifteen percent increase. The second offer was at a larger company with forty percent higher compensation, but a less senior-sounding title, at least on paper. Both companies and offers aligned with her core values. Do you want to guess what she chose? Consistent with her primacy, Andrea took the higher paying offer with the less-impressive sounding title. She saw this position as more valuable for salary progression whether she stayed or moved on at a later time. This decision helped with early retirement goals—a topic of serious concern, since Andrea's partner was twelve years her senior. It can seem so simple and straightforward reading the example in hindsight, but in the moment, these can be stressful decisions that tear at high performers.

Primacy Pathing is a great next step for you if you're facing typical high-performer dilemmas, similar to the following:

- Should I focus on a specific industry or be a functional expert?
- Should I go back to school?
- Should I change companies? Change roles?
- Should I take a leave of absence? Go part time? Stop working?
- Should I return to work?
- Should I launch my own business?
- Should I take that international assignment? Relocate?
- Should I take that promotion? Should I take the demotion?

The answer to all these questions is another question (the classic consulting answer): It depends; what has primacy for you at this moment in time? A coach helps provide clarity and illuminates inconsistencies or self-limiting beliefs as you address the primacy questions, but only you can decide what is most important at this time. And remember, when faced with the big decisions and tradeoffs, stay grounded in your core values.

Primacy Pathing Tool #2: Your Ideal Day

I grew up in a family business that manufactured medical examination tables, the wooden kind with the fake leather top. Some models were simple rectangles, some had a hole cut out for your face (for the proctologists), some had stirrups, and some raised up and down. When I was younger, I'd help write shipping labels and sweep sawdust. When I was a bit taller, I'd stand on blocks at the drill press to make holes in table legs for the screws. I liked watching the threads of wood come out of the drilled holes like curly fries. To this day, fresh-cut sawdust provides a powerful sense memory for me.

When I could be trusted more with power tools and accuracy, I staple-gunned and glued, along with the full-time employees. I watched my dad teach a nineteen-year-old high school dropout how to read a calendar to schedule shipments. Mom ran the office in the early days of the business, treating every customer like they were the only one we had. I watched my parents go to this work they loved every day. After work, Mom, Dad, my brother, and I were all required to be at the dinner table for supper. Mom cooked dinner every night, often vegetables from the garden or fresh-caught bass and bream.

My father and I had a special, close relationship, and we both got the giggles at awkward moments. Once my baby brother came streaking, screaming out of the shower with a shampoo bottle swinging from his bottom lip. He had flipped open the bottle with his teeth. Suction formed somehow and sucked his bottom lip into the bottle cap. While brother Mike was crying in pain and Mom was on the cusp of calling an ambulance, Dad and I ran down the hall to giggle as quietly as we could because that scene was just too funny to bear stone-faced seriousness. We also loved to share obscure vocabulary words. We called stomach growling borborygmi and body odor hircus. He helped me study for every test. So what does all this have to do with executive coaching?

One day, while riding home from school with Dad, heading back to the shop, I asked him what his ideal day was. This question related to a creative writing assignment for which I had to write a story about *my* ideal day.

He said, "Every day is my ideal day."

"You're joking!" I said, with the annoying smirk of a pre-teen.

"Every day, I get to do what I want to do," he explained. "I don't know a lot of people who can say that."

I was too young to understand that second part about other people, but I heard what he said, "Every day is my ideal day. Every day I get to do what I want to do."

Certainly, much of your ideal day is mindset, but the reality is that there are aspects of your day you control. That's where you should focus your efforts, controlling the controllables to make the time for what has primacy. A powerful place to start is by defining your ideal day. Literally.

What does your ideal day look like, feel like, sound like, smell like from the moment you wake up to the time you go to sleep? Some people articulate their ideal day as a timed agenda. From 7:00 a.m. to 7:30 a.m., I work out. From 7:30 a.m to 8:00 a.m., I check emails. And so forth. Others use drawings to depict themselves in their ideal activities. For example, here I am walking at the end of the day with my spouse. Here is my family all at the dinner table. Here I am giving a great presentation. One client used cutouts and taped images to convey her ideal day. Another client wrote an original song inspired by how his ideal day ebbs and flows and feels. He played it for me on the piano, and I understood that day perfectly. Are you ready to describe your ideal day? Grab the worksheet at www.the-me-suite.com/tools.

Step 1: Whether you're more literal or conceptual, articulate the features in your ideal day in the language that speaks to you.

Consider:

- What are your sacred routines? Think of these as activities or behaviors that, when missed, make you feel "off" or resentful.
- What relationships do you nurture and how?
- What alone time do you have?
- What value are you adding to others?
- What are you saying no to?

Step 2: For each of the above daily routines, assign a percentage of time for which that activity is present in your ideal day. If you're satisfied with that percentage, great. If you're not, ask these critical questions: "What is in my control that I could change?" and "For the things that are in my control, how much do I want to make a change?" You may be okay having the ideal day once a month or a few times a year. That's your option. Just be intentional about the decision.

I learned a twist on Your Ideal Day from a client, Nic, a confessed Hamster-Wheel Hank. Nic took the seven dimensions from Primacy Pathing to decide what role each would play in his ideal day. He took this even further to design his ideal week with specific commitments for each Primacy Pathing dimension.

Nic's ideal week:

1. Career: Learn something every month that I didn't know.
2. Finances: Stick to the budget and savings plan.
3. Family: Breakfast with the kids 2x.
4. Health: Peloton 3x.
5. Personal Growth: Pick up the guitar at least once.
6. Spirituality: Take an evening nature walk with my partner 2x.
7. Relationships: Send a handwritten thank-you note every Friday.

A Crossroads K.T. client used the Ideal Day exercise to decide which job offer to accept. K.T. was recently divorced and wanted the flexibility to be present with the kids for homework and ball games. Being clear about this primacy eliminated one offer that would require early morning and late-night conference calls with clients in Asia. This K.T. used the Ideal Day to map which job offer best supported the elements in their ideal day.

An Exploration Erika client used the Ideal Day to address a dilemma. "I'm no longer taking care of a sick relative. I now have about eight extra hours a week. How do I want to focus this newfound time?" This Erika decided that most dimensions were running along just fine—keep them as is—so Erika made the decision to double down on personal growth and begin cooking classes and Mandarin classes online. This Erika commented, "Painting my ideal day helped me prioritize the classes I wanted to take without feeling guilty that something else was needing that time."

Primacy Pathing Tool #3: Your Ideal Job Description

In business, the best indication that a strategy is clear is that knowing what to say no to is obvious. When my clients know what to say no to, I count that as a victory *par excellence*. For high performers in career search mode—whether in an external search, internal role move with their existing employer, or launching a business—having a strategy is critical. The strategy helps create options. The same is true across all dimensions of your life.

High performers struggle with the sea of opportunities. They see possibilities everywhere. They are curious. They catch on quickly. They are choosy, but they also don't want to shut off a discussion that might go somewhere. If they are currently in between jobs, the stress, doubt, and sense of urgency can be paralyzing. This is where writing your Ideal Job Description can be a powerful primacy tool.

Reflect on two simple questions:

1. "What would have to be true about a job offer (or new role) for me to say yes to it immediately? I'd stop looking immediately if these things were true."

Consider:

- Vision, mission, core values
- Role, title, compensation, benefits
- Hours, location, and travel
- Mentor, boss, team
- Autonomy
- Degree of stretch and learning

2. Conversely, "What are my no-ways?"

   Consider:

   - I will not take a role for less than $X.
   - I will not work in ____ industry.
   - I would never work for ____.
   - I won't move to ____.
   - I won't sit at a desk for____ hours.
   - Other

Remember: primacy is about what's most important at this moment. Expect your primacy to change or evolve over time. Just as companies refresh their business priorities based on what's happening in the market, you must refresh your primacy based on what's happening in your life. Most often, when my clients are struggling with a big decision, it's because they haven't looked their primacy in the face. Expect naming your primacy to require some hard thinking, to make your brain a little sore. Expect some self-reflection debates and surprises. It's rewarding work and often hard.

Your Career Is Like a Tomato

As a gardener, I see career analogies in every seed planted, every flower pollinated, every fruit ripening. Tomatoes present the biggest dilemma. Do I let that beauty ripen to summer perfection on the vine and risk squirrel sabotage, or do I pick it now, letting it ripen safely in the kitchen in a paper bag, yielding more of a grocery store flavor? Similar to the great tomato dilemma, my clients often wrestle with picking just the right moments in their career, and you likely do as well. Should you stay to ripen fully on the vine where you are or ripen elsewhere? High performers, by nature, wrestle with the fundamental dilemmas of "What if?" and "Is now the time?"

Ask yourself if any of these sound familiar:

- Everyone knows me as an expert in X, but I want to do Y.
- I'm pretty content where I am right now. Should I explore new job opportunities to test my market value?
- Should I stay in my current role, hoping for promotion this year, or do I take the interesting new offer I just got?
- Should I take the offer I have right now or wait for something more perfect to come along?
- Can I take a leave of absence without stunting my career?
- Do I need to stay in this function/industry where I'm an expert, or can I be relevant in other areas where I have an interest in growing?
- I don't want to change companies, but that seems like the fastest way to advance my title and pay.

These are fortunate problems, but they can be stressful and distracting. Do the work to identify your primacy. Your career is like a tomato. You have to pick the right time.

Personal Brand: What People Think and Feel When They Hear Your Name

What do you think and feel when you read these names?

Adidas and Nike. Airbnb and Marriott. Apple and Samsung. Ford and Hyundai. Paris and Tokyo.

The thoughts and feelings that came to mind as you read these names make up your perception of their brand. The same thing happens when people hear or read your name. They have thoughts and feelings about you when they see and hear your name, and those thoughts and feelings comprise your personal brand.

Personal branding is a hot topic in the age of social media. Books, blogs, and courses abound. We all intellectually understand what a personal brand is, but we often feel it manipulative and inauthentic to *manage* our personal brand. Think of your personal brand like a body—a physical human body. We all have one. We can either nurture that body so it does what we want it to do, or we can ignore it and just let it go, limping along after years of neglect. Whether we nurture the body or ignore the body, we still have a body. The question to ask yourself is: "Is this body in service of what I want?" Your personal brand is similar. You have a personal brand right now, whether you want one or not, so cultivate it deliberately to be in service of what you want.

My client, Robert (a Hamster-Wheel Hank), wanted to move into corporate strategy roles, but his last ten years had been in human resources with talent acquisition and succession planning. Everyone thought of him as only on an HR path, so he started an external job search out of frustration. He felt trapped with no other options. In our work together, including a personal branding survey and self-reflection exercises, Robert learned he had a strong personal brand for identifying the right talent for the role, conducting analytics to drive decisions, and keeping people calm and engaged during stressful times. We worked to signal to higher-ups how those strong personal-brand elements were relevant to the company's corporate strategy, which was to grow through acquisitions. Robert moved from HR to the Chief Strategy Officer's team, conducting due diligence for the acquisition integration planning. He didn't have to change companies to do the work he wanted to do, but he did have to pivot his brand in the minds of others—and in his own mind.

Another client was struggling to get promoted to the senior level. Dani, a Crossroads K.T., had been pleased with her trajectory for many years. As her boss excelled, so did she. At each of the boss's promotions, he pulled Dani along the ladder at the rung just below. When he got promoted to his next level, she got promoted to her next level. This played out several times and was terrific, until the moment Dani was ready to leapfrog. She didn't need to be in the wake of the boss's rise anymore. She was ready for promotion, to be the peer of that boss, and she knew it. But she feared her personal brand was stuck in the shadow as the assist. At the same time, she had an attractive offer from another company that would give her the promotion bump she was ready for, but she didn't want to start over with the competitor if she didn't have to.

The first thing Dani and I worked on was primacy, and she clearly defined her primacy as getting promoted as quickly as possible. Such clarity is gold in coaching. Dani then launched three discussions with her key leaders to understand the perceptions of her personal brand and readiness for promotion. She forced the conversation, revealing she had a competitive offer and communicating her expectations for promotion. Leaders at her company were surprised in these discussions—surprised at how strong her promotion-readiness story was and surprised at how boldly she was seeking the promotion. Through the conversations, she secured a champion who was eager to move her into another part of the organization where they had an open role for her that would yield a promotion within the current cycle. Dani's personal brand moved from second-chair descriptors like high potential, reliable, flexible, quick learner, and supportive, to first-chair descriptors like high performer, strategic, leader, owner-mindset, and hungry for more.

> No one will ever care about your career as much as you do, so own it.

If you think this approach was tricky, you're right. First, Dani needed a strong network she could approach with her promotion-readiness story. Second, she had to trust the advice given and promises made. Third, she had to not alienate the boss who had been so pivotal in her numerous promotions, to position him as her advocate. Finally, the progression might not have gone this smoothly had she not already had the competitive offer as leverage. Dani put in the work to own her next best career move at the crossroads. This was not through manipulative personal branding. It was not through inauthentic personal branding. It was by pivoting her personal brand from passenger to driver. She achieved her primacy. She stayed at the company and got the promised promotion.

Conduct your own personal branding exercise. First, write down the top five words that come to mind that describe your personal brand. Don't share this list with others.

Then, ask eight to ten people in your life to do the same exercise. Have each person write down the top five words that come to mind when they hear your name. Choose a combination of people from your professional and personal life. (For the people from your professional life, select those who have worked closely with you for three months or more.)

Next, gather all the lists, and look for synonyms or similar concepts where words could be clustered or combined. This will inform your personal brand today. Decide if your current personal brand signals what you want for yourself in the future. If it does not, the work now begins with the networking, skills and strengths, and storytelling focus areas below.

In the hundreds of times I've coached this exercise, a few themes invariably emerge. The same might be true for you.

Common themes include:

- You'll be shocked at how similar the lists are.
- Two or three words people have used will surprise you and make you proud.
- A few words people share might make you cringe. One podcast guest on *The Me-Suite* podcast often hears he's "nice." While it's nice to be nice, he's pivoted his brand as a leader to "fair" and "trusted."
- You'll value this exercise, as it'll inform how you show up.
- Those you asked will be thrilled to participate and will want to do it for themselves too.

I have significantly pivoted my brand four times. Two times required me to return to school to signal a new brand with a reset diploma button. One case was my choice to pursue an MBA when I was switching from professional acting to business. The second case was when I left management consulting as a senior partner and secured an executive coaching diploma and launched The Me-Suite. The other two personal branding pivots were internal at the same company. The first was when I was known for culture and change and needed to expand my brand to include more quantitative prowess to secure a senior P&L position. The other was when I needed to progress with the times and demonstrate more digital mindedness. In both cases, I latched on to and shadowed a mentor until the training wheels fell off.

Remember: you have a personal brand whether you want one or not. Manage it, or others will. Think of your personal brand as a signaling device. It signals who you are, what you do, and what you want to do. Manage your personal brand—what people think and feel when they hear your name—to attract what you want to attract.

Personal Branding and Job Interviewing

Personal branding takes on heightened significance when you explore a new job opportunity or seek a new role within your existing organization. I've interviewed over one thousand candidates as a hiring executive. I've prepped hundreds as a certified career coach. Although these tips benefit high performers across all career stages, you may be surprised that this topic is one of my most-requested areas of support for senior professionals. Personal storytelling is hard. High performers prioritize its value, and they practice. Here are my top three interviewing tips for external job searching, internal role changes, and start-up pitches.

First, demonstrate that you're running *to* something not *from* something. Leave negativity out of it. Recruiters and hiring managers are like horses; they can small fear. If you tell negative stories or talk about what's wrong with the place you want to leave, you send signals to the interviewers that something may be off. You plant a seed of doubt that the issues may actually be with *you*. Prepare thoughtfully any stories you want to tell that cast a negative light on your current or previous employment. Focus your preparation and energy on what you want to attract, not what you want to leave behind. Run *to* the new role, not *from* the old one.

Next, control your narrative when an interviewer asks any of the following:

- Tell me about yourself. Walk me through your resume.
- Why have you decided to leave your current position?
- What interests you in this company/this role?
- Why are you a good fit for this role?

Always be prepared to answer and crystallize your messages around "why this role, why me, why now," and you'll be ready for just about anything.

Finally, don't ask lazy questions. Lazy questions are the ones interviewers hear over and over and which don't require much prep on your part. These questions are boring for the interviewer and non-differentiating for you.

Lazy questions include:

- What is the culture like here?
- How did you decide to come work here? (Or what's kept you here all these years?)
- What do you like most about working here?
- If you had a magic wand to change one thing about working here, what would it be?

Prepare more thoughtful, insightful questions that demonstrate you've done some work, such as these questions:

- I saw the recent acquisition announcement. What excites you most about that opportunity for customers? For employees?
- Are there any experiences this role requires that I haven't touched on in my examples so far? Any areas you'd like to explore more?

Do the work. What can you learn about the personal brand and core values of your interviewer to craft informed, tailored questions?

Personal Branding While Remote

Being remote isn't remotely like being in person. While the pandemic has made onscreen engagement second nature, familiarity isn't mastery and often entices sloppiness. Do not underestimate the challenge of presenting yourself and engaging onscreen. It's a different art form to master at all levels. These tips apply broadly to onscreen interactions where the stakes are highest, such as interviewing with a new company, seeking a meaningful move within your current company, pitching to a new customer or venture capital firm, or giving and receiving performance feedback. The more experienced you are at presenting in person, the more you may need these reminders. Consider these important elements of your onscreen presence as you prepare for that important remote interaction.

Look at yourself. Record yourself in advance to master your environment. Check the camera angle, height, and distance. Are your face and shoulders properly in the frame? Are you cut off at the chin? Can I see you need to trim your nose hair? In one client pitch, the presenter was so close to the screen, we saw only eyes, nose, and mouth like a face smashed into a magnifying glass. I am sure the presenter was saying smart things, but the fishbowl effect distracted from the content, and no one knew her well enough to interrupt and ask that she adjust the camera angle. Another favorite is the talking propeller-head. You know, the presenter or interviewee positioned perfectly in the room so the ceiling fan is coming straight out of their head. If you were meeting in person, you wouldn't block the office door with your chair, so don't have the ceiling fan coming out of the top of your head.

Be thoughtful about your eye contact tendencies. Understand how others interpret your gaze. It's difficult to emulate the directness of in-person eye contact with computer cameras, and everyone understands that. At the same time, eyes moving about are distracting and suggest you're multitasking even when you're not. If you're using two monitors, let people know so they understand why you're looking away. If you look down to take notes, let people know. Otherwise, you may appear to be texting with someone more important. This is similar to texting under the table in an in-person meeting. Be extra careful about looking away with a grin. In groups, this can indicate you just read a humorous private chat, which is annoying and disrespectful to the presenter, just like passing notes or whispering in an in-person setting.

Your intention manifests in your posture. If your intention is to have a casual touchpoint with a colleague, your posture will be relaxed, perhaps slumping a bit, wearing a t-shirt, nursing a water bottle. If you want to project authority over a topic, your seated posture will be upright and leaning in. If you use a standing desk, check that you don't sway or rock. Plant both feet flat on the ground for a commanding presence.

Be mindful of your sound quality with and without a headset. Record yourself and have a practice onscreen call with a friend to test the quality of your audio. You may find you're wearing the headset mic too close to your mouth so your sound is distorted. You may hear an echo or ambient noise. If you were presenting in person, you'd probably go to the room in advance to test the projector, the screen, the lapel mic. Give your important onscreen interactions the same attention. Be careful that your familiarity with onscreen interactions doesn't lead to less thoughtfulness in the brand you want to convey.

Prepare for the question traps that worsen on video. Most interviews start with innocent questions that are often time-sucking traps, especially on video when you can't easily interrupt people or read body language. *Do not interpret these questions literally.* Instead, share your unique story by summarizing the themes that flow through the arc of your career, themes that brought you to today and make you uniquely relevant for this new role. Be prepared to take control of your narrative any time you hear: "Tell me about yourself," "Walk me through your resume," or "How did you become interested in this position?" This takes practice, so practice.

Find ways to engage like a three-dimensional human being. You may find it relevant to display a logo if you share the same alma mater as your interviewer, for example. Be creative and intentional. Do your research, and be thoughtful in the questions you ask. Challenge your preparation by asking yourself, "Could I ask this question of any company, or have I tailored questions thoughtfully to this particular interview based on my knowledge of the company, the role, the interviewer?" And finally, smile. Go in with the mindset that the interviewer is on your side. Remember, interviewers want you to be "the one." They are very rarely trying to trick you and catch you doing something wrong. They are hoping you're the perfect candidate because if you are, their job is so much easier. The interviewer is most often on your side until you give them a reason not to be.

Set the tone by considering how the interviewer should feel. Select a background or setting that supports your personal brand. Decide what you want your onscreen background to signal, whether it's your physical space or a virtual background you've selected. In the beginning of the pandemic, I used virtual backgrounds because my back wall was so stark. I then nailed up diplomas to signal credentials to new clients, but the display looked like a stuffy office from the eighties. I now have a simple piece of art that adds a little color without being distracting.

Dress according to your personal brand. Yes, you've been working through the era of the dress shirt paired with sweatpants—business on top, gym on the bottom—but for those most important interactions, show up onscreen as you would in person. Use lighting that keeps you bright and in focus. A ring light is the easiest solution.

Install blinds if you need to adjust the sun exposure throughout the day. Whether real or virtual, your environment sets a tone, so be deliberate in your choices.

Let logistics work *for* you, not *against* you. Ensure stable Wi-Fi. (It's shocking how much this is still an issue.) Show up with fully charged batteries. (A senior vice president client had to reschedule an interview because his earbud batteries died.) Agree on a contingency plan for technology failures, such as knowing the interviewer's email and cell for last-minute issues. Prepare by accessing the interviewer's video link in advance to check your settings. Have your mobile phone handy for backup.

Minimize outdoor and indoor noises that could distract and present a poor impression by planning for quiet and solitude. Consider rescheduling the leaf-blowing and sending the pet to daycare if the stakes are that high. In contrast, you may want the pet in view, sleeping by your side or crawling across your screen, to signal who you are and what you're about. Again, there is no right answer, but it is wrong to not be intentional. You can't control all the variables, and companies are rightfully giving everyone so much more grace these days, but plan what you can.

You get one chance to make a first impression, and often that is a virtual one these days, so be intentional in all you do.

Signaling Your Personal Brand on Social Media

Your personal brand is not only what people think and feel when they hear your name. It is also what you signal via your social media presence. For the purposes of career strategies, I'll focus here on LinkedIn, but the lessons apply to other social media platforms and even to the way you email and text.

Too often, leaders use LinkedIn as an electronic resume, when, instead, it should be used as a signaling device to attract what you want to attract in your life. Think about the important meaning behind the word signal.

Signal: *(verb)* to indicate with special meaning.

Signal: *(noun)* a stimulus to which someone responds.

Signal: *(adj.)* distinguished from the ordinary.

You spend a lot of energy creating your LinkedIn profile, parading the facts in the "Experience" section. This is often simply a cut and paste from your traditional resume, isn't it? For example, "I worked there from time x to y. And then I went to work here. I completed this degree." This is static, lazy content, not *signaling* content. What is your LinkedIn profile signaling right now? Is it attracting what you want to attract?

Assess the following:

- What *value* are you bringing?
- How do others perceive your *personal brand*?
- Will a potential customer see your *differentiation*?
- Can a recruiter find your *special sauce*?
- Are you *relevant* to the field you want to play in?

Make time to refresh your LinkedIn profile. Shine a strategic light on:

- The style of your photo and banner. What look and feel conveys your brand?
- The words underneath your photo. Does this convey the value you bring, or is it simply a job title few will understand?
- About: If someone read no further, what impression would this section make?

- Activity: What is your strategy for liking, sharing, and posting content (type, frequency)? This strategy is most underappreciated.
- Endorsements: Is this list fresh and relevant?
- Recommendations: How can this area help you? Reach out to four people and request they write you a recommendation around your target signal area.
- Volunteering: Where do you give back? What causes do you support?
- Accomplishments: Name your differentiators.
- Interests: Be deliberate in what people and content you follow. This signals where you get your information.

Remember, regardless of the social media channel, you aren't signaling if there's no one on the other side to receive the signal, so grow your network one authentic connection at a time. You'll learn more on this in the Relationships chapter that follows.

Take Headhunter Calls to Signal and Practice Your Brand

At my first consulting job out of business school, the lead partner called me into his office on day one. He started with the expected: "Welcome to the firm. We're excited to have you." That felt great. Then, quickly came the surprise. "Donna, I want you to keep your resume up to date, and take headhunter phone calls."

Oh, crap. This made for an interesting first few months. I was worried that either the company was going down or I didn't have what it takes. I later realized the two gifts the partner gave me that day. First, an updated, current resume reflects where you've grown and where you want to grow. You're signaling your personal brand and identifying the next best move you want to pursue for professional growth, internally or externally, now or later. Second, taking headhunter calls with some frequency tests your relevance and value in the market, while allowing you to practice your storytelling skills.

Yes, the resume and headhunter efforts take some time and preparation. Here's why these efforts are worth prioritizing. First, if you decide to stay where you are, you stay confidently and invested. You don't have to wonder "what if?" You know what the "if" is, and you've made the choice to stay, willingly and selectively, from a position of strength. You aren't stuck because of lack of choices or simply because of your own inertia. Second, if you decide to make a change, or are forced to make one, you're at the ready. You aren't stale. You aren't delayed. You aren't scrambling to remember what should be on your resume. You aren't relearning how to interview and tell your unique story. You're informed and prepared.

One year, I was up for a milestone promotion, and I thought I was going to make it. I didn't. I was pissed. My mojo was drained. I went to a negative place and checked out a bit. I started taking headhunter phone calls and realized there wasn't anything terribly compelling that I wanted to run toward outside of the company where I was. So after exploring the "what ifs," I made the choice to stay. The operative words here are "I made the choice." I wasn't trapped. I was in control of my next best move. I was promoted the next year.

When was the last time you refreshed your resume? Your LinkedIn profile? When is the last headhunter call you took to practice your messaging and test the market? When you're creating growth plans for those around you, don't forget to create one for yourself.

Relationships: Keep Your Network Deposits and Withdrawals in Balance

In years past, managing my network wasn't my strong suit. I was so poor at this discipline and missed so many opportunities to help others and be helped myself. I've completed college and three master's-level programs at premier institutions. I am actively in touch with maybe twenty individuals across those experiences. I could easily email former classmates, and they will eagerly respond, but I'd have to first remind them who I am and how we met and hope they'd remember me. It's embarrassing.

So many clients I supported when they were green, newbies in their jobs, are now senior executives whose emails and phone numbers I didn't keep. Certainly, social media is helping leaders keep track of people's whereabouts and milestone events, but you have to first be grounded in a relationship strategy to make that online outreach work for you. You have to be intentional about the deposits and withdrawals you want to make in those relationships. As with anything that matters, this takes work.

In business, high performers typically talk more about our networks and less about our relationships. When you focus on the desired outcome of networking—quality relationships—you network to build relationships, understanding that all relationships are in your network, but not all networks are relationships. I have come across many people in my life who want to reject networking as something slimy. I agree that networking is slimy if it's all about engaging only when you need something. But networking is the beginning of forming quality relationships nurtured with intentionality. The higher the quality of the relationships in your life, the more options you'll have.

Think about someone in your life whom you respect as a champion networker. How do they show up? What do they do that impresses you the most? Are they like your colleague Liz, who sends the happy birthday note each year, even three years after you last worked together? Are they like Lee, who hunts you down to introduce you to someone helpful to know in your field? Maybe they show up like Ravi, who sends a $5 Starbucks card when he hears you got promoted or just joined his team.

Now that I've upped my relationship game, I deploy my favorite relationship-building strategy: "Think You. Tell You." I read the Sunday *New York Times* religiously, old school, on paper, every week. When an article reminds me of someone, I stop to share it with the person with a quick note saying, "Thought of you." For example, one client advocates plant-based foods, so I sent her the interview with Beyond Meat's CEO. A colleague was exploring data science certifications, so I forwarded a column on workplace trends. A friend works in the non-profit sector, so I snapped a photo of a relevant new book on charitable giving trends post-COVID. If the article makes me think of you, I will tell you, right then. That's the relationship-building commitment I make to myself. Making deposits into the relationship account.

Creating options in your life requires surrounding yourself with the right people, intentionally building relationships, and putting your network to work for you. This requires inventorying and nurturing current relationships and identifying the relationships you don't have and need to build. Think about your network like a water fountain. You need to both hydrate and refill the tank. Sometimes you are the one hydrating, taking water from the relationship fountain. You need help with job interviewing or an introduction, for example. Sometimes you're the one bringing the fresh water to refill the tank, pouring into the relationship fountain by reviewing a resume or helping someone get a referral. The goal is to not let the relationship fountain run dry. For the more analytically minded reader, think of a relationship like a bank account. This account needs to be balanced. Sometimes you have a need, and you make withdrawals. Sometimes you help others by making deposits.

If you're Exploration Erika, relationship withdrawals help you brainstorm, learn, test ideas. They can introduce you to others in your areas of interest. If you're Crossroads K.T., relationship withdrawals can include contacting mentors or coaches who help you size up the pros and cons of a big decision. They can help you think through your blind spots or help keep you honest about your core values and primacy. If you're Hamster-Wheel Hank, relationship withdrawals are very similar to those for Exploration Erika. The difference is often in mindset. With Exploration Erika, the glass is likely half full, curious about the possibilities, like a dog out for a walk, sniffing every little thing with excitement. With Hamster-Wheel Hank, the relationship withdrawals often provide the much-needed positive energy to propel you to your next best move, helping to get the sleepy dog off the sofa to go take that walk. Whether you're Exploration Erika, Crossroads K.T., or Hamster-Wheel Hank, the quality of your relationship withdrawals will be commensurate with the quality of your relationship deposits. Relationships go both ways.

Conduct Your Relationship Inventory

One of the most rewarding exercises you can invest in is a Relationship Inventory. By studying and categorizing all the diverse players currently in your orbit, you'll illuminate a whole universe of advice, introductions, and referrals that are only an email, a text, or a door knock away. Here's a great place to start.

Relationship Inventory

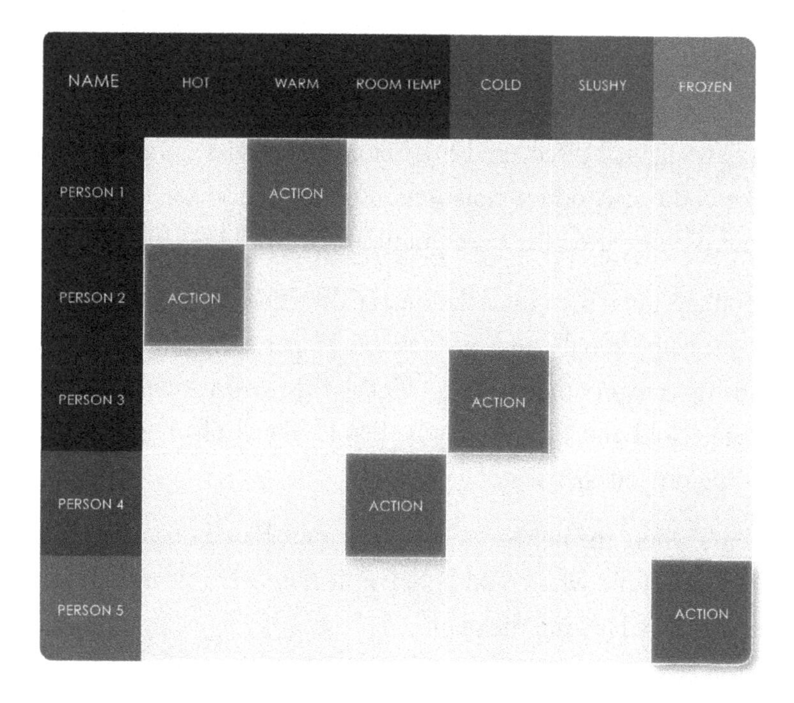

Create six relationship category columns in an Excel grid or some other sortable format. Hot connections are people you can text right now, and they'll text right back, likely with an emoji. Warm contacts are those you haven't connected with in a while, but a message from you by email would feel natural and welcome. The Room Temp people might need a slight nudge to remember you. You'll be remembered with neutral-to-positive emotions. Those in the Cold category are people connected to you through a common experience (alumni network, clubs, associations). They don't know you personally, but they are prewired to want to network with you.

You don't know the Slushy people and have no natural connection to them, but a connection would be valuable. Networking would require a creative approach to get their attention. Those in the Frozen category represent relationships with burned bridges. Acknowledge the risk they may pose. For example, if you're seeking a new customer or a new job, could this person speak negatively about you and hurt your odds? Is this a personal relationship that shakes your confidence with negativity? Be honest with yourself about any relationship that sits in this category and seek to neutralize their influence. Once, while preparing a pitch for work with a new client, I discovered a decision-maker was someone I had once fired for code-of-conduct violations. For that reason, I helped prep the team but did not attend the presentation.

Populate rows in your Relationship Inventory Grid with the names from your personal and professional networks, indicating what relationship category they fall into. Get all the names down; don't edit. (At this stage, Cold and Slushy may be blank. You'll fill them in over time, depending on your networking goals.)

Here's where the networking work begins. Based on your career goals, identify the people who could help you if they were aware of your goals. Develop a plan. Execute the plan.

Consider these tips if you find networking a tad awkward:

- People like to help people. (Remember how good it feels when people ask you for your advice and support.)
- You can help by introducing two people in your network to each other.
- Close the discussion with: "Thank you. Is there anything I can do to help you?"

In 2020, I had to put my network to work overtime as I launched *The Me-Suite* podcast and sought weekly guests to interview. I prepared my relationship inventory and targeted the individuals I thought best fit my podcast purpose and would also embrace the social media actions required for success. I was admittedly a little nervous reaching out. First, I was asking people to commit about two hours of their time with no compensation. Second, I was asking them to offer their personal brand to participate in something unknown. *The Me-Suite* podcast was just an idea with some audio files on a laptop. It didn't yet have any accolades to boost confidence and entice a guest to participate.

Hesitantly, I contacted Kris via email. She was a C-suite executive in the diversity, equity, and inclusion (DE&I) space, and I was producing an episode about leadership and social justice. I feared reaching out to Kris might drain the relationship fountain, asking her for more than I could give in return. In my note, I even gave her "a graceful exit," option. She could select, "Now is not a good time. Thank you for considering me."

Fast forward, and Kris was thrilled to hear from me and felt the moon and stars had aligned when she got my note. She had been actively exploring opportunities to grow her presence in the market as a DE&I leader, seeking platforms to engage in dialogue and share her points of view and expertise. This was a true win-win that would not have happened had I not put my network to work.

Tips for Balancing the Relationship Accounts

- Be there. Congratulate and support others in their moments that matter. (Hint: Simple likes and shares are a great place to start.)
- Be relevant. Share ideas, articles, and introductions that support others' interests. (Hint: When you see something that reminds you of someone, act on that, and let them know.)
- Say "thank you," often.
- Make more deposits than withdrawals. (Hint: This isn't about keeping tabs; it's about having a mindset of helpfulness.)
- Be intentional. Choose to bring into your life people who are supportive of your core values and goals. Shed those who are toxic. This may mean shedding some family members, and I'm so sorry if it does. I've been there.

Recognize some people are weeds.

A weed is interference—a plant that is harmful, not helpful. For example, although we love mint and dandelions under many circumstances, they can quickly choke other plants out of sunlight and nutrients if not managed. In contrast, some plants are complements that enhance the other plants around them. Marigolds are terrific to place with tomatoes since the marigolds emit a chemical that wards off nematodes. Marigolds even help repel mosquitoes. So it goes with people.

Some people in our networks are weeds. Some are marigolds. "Weed people" crowd others out to get noticed. They do more taking than giving. They use "I" most of the time, even though "weed" starts with "we." Marigold people, on the other hand, contribute positively to any environment. They embrace collaboration and believe everyone in the ecosystem has a unique contribution to be valued. Think of your network as a garden of people, rows and rows of personal and professional connections you allow to take root in your life in some way. Survey which people are the marigolds you want to cultivate and which are the weeds you need to pull. Cultivate your networks. Do your weed-eating. Tend your people garden.

There is nothing we accomplish truly alone. Nothing. Is there someone you've been meaning to connect with? Do it this week.

Check out more networking tips (including How to Make Networking Feel Less Slimy) and an example of the Relationship Inventory Grid at www.the-me-suite.com/tools.

Skills and Strengths: Think Creatively and Broadly About the Value You Bring

I was the student teachers wanted in class. I sat still. I did my homework on time. I participated without dominating. I got straight As. A as in Always. As a young learner, I colored inside the lines. As a high schooler, I kept off the grass. In college, I played to my strengths.

If I'm ever offered time travel, I will start my do-over around ninth grade with one mantra: "Donna, make straight Cs." I will pick topics because they are interesting, not because I can test well in them. I will seek classes that intimidate me. I will register for courses people would find surprising. I will measure myself on a "growth card," rather than on a report card. Getting straight Cs will be the sweet spot on the growth card. Straight Cs will symbolize how much I embrace learning something difficult. How well I balance taking a risk on something really new while applying the effort required to learn it. And while I'm back there in time, I'll also advise my younger self to keep the perm in the past and lighten up on the eyeliner.

My desire to make straight As had me thinking very narrowly about my skills and strengths. I stayed in one lane for a long time. It wasn't until I started getting compliments on my communications skills in business that I realized the power of thinking more broadly and creatively about the value I bring. I now excel at helping others explore how today's skills and strengths are applicable in exciting, new areas. I help them clarify opportunities where they want to develop, grow, and expand.

Thinking broadly and creatively (what I call fungibly) about your skills and strengths gives you options. High performers are very good at asking, "What do you do?" or "What's your role?" The answer, however, is often too literal.

Although these statements may be factual, they are too narrow. You should instead be talking about the types of problems you solve and the value you deliver. For example, if you're an accountant, you are likely also good at broader skills, such as finding patterns, making order out of chaos, and paying attention to detail. If you're a marketer, you aren't just pitching and selling. You're likely also good at broader, fungible skills, such as market segmentation, customer insights, design thinking, and making tradeoff decisions. If you work in operations, you are good at process and execution and likely look for solutions end to end, understanding interdependencies. You are also likely creative with continuous improvement, issue resolution, and team motivation.

When I was preparing for interviews in business school, some people in the careers office expected that, given my acting background, I would not be a contender for the strategy consulting firms. Indeed, most firms I interviewed with did not select me first. I had to use the points system to work my way on to the interview list, like a walk-on in sports. However, I did the hard work of thinking broadly and creatively about my theatre training and how a strategy consulting firm would benefit from those skills. I told stories of how I'd spent about ten years putting myself in the shoes of others to see challenges from their point of view, to understand why they think as they do, how they communicate, how they relate to others.

Consultants need to influence people through compelling evidence and communication to move the client to a decision or action. I demonstrated to the interviewers that this acting skill, at its core, offers the differentiated empathy and influence required for client change. Indeed, the strategy consulting job I landed was the highest paying one across all firms on campus that year. (I used to joke that my theatre skills continued to help me act like I knew what I was doing a lot of the time.) If my acting skills can prove fungible to a strategy consulting career, you've got this. Don't be so literal. Your skills are more transferrable than you realize.

Many career people narrow what they're known for and what they're good at. They don't think broadly about how transferable some of their experiences can be in other roles, other industries.

To dive into your skills and strengths with the fungibility and creativity frame of mind:

1. Assess your skills and strengths across the three dimensions (interpersonal, functional, and technical).

2. Step back and look at your skills agnostic of the industry, the role, or the organization where you currently reside.
3. Investigate the role descriptions for the type of work you want to do, and map that against your skills-and-strengths assessment.
4. Identify the new skills you may want to build in service of your interests and goals.

This exercise will give you a realistic view of where you have transferrable skills that others will immediately understand with proper storytelling, and where you have skills gaps that need to be filled through technical training, certifications, or more formal education. Assessment tools such as StrengthsFinder, DISC, Birkman, DNA Behavior, Working Genius, and others are helpful in heightening your understanding of your natural strengths under both comfortable and stressed conditions. They are also helpful in giving you a vocabulary as you start to think more broadly and creatively about where your skills and strengths could add value.

Interpersonal	Functional	Technical
Communication	Budgeting / Forecasting	Industry Knowledge
Conflict Resolution	Business Planning	Licenses
Mentoring	Data Science	Software Experience
Negotiation	Sales and Marketing	Specialized Training
Influence	Logistics	Degrees/Certifications
Collaboration	Program Management	Language Proficiency
Etc.	Etc.	Etc.

Let's consider how my client, Manny, thought creatively about his skills and strengths. Manny is an accountant who was feeling like an Exploration Erika, Crossroads K.T., and Hamster-Wheel Hank all in one. As a CPA, he is an expert in the field of accounting and financial reporting. He pursued this field in college more by default than by design, as many of us do. He is also, by nature, a puzzle-solver who enjoys finding out how all the pieces of unstructured data fit together to tell a story. He recognizes patterns and deviations from patterns. He enjoys forensic activities that get to the root of inconsistencies or trends in data. He appreciates details and accuracy. But Manny didn't want to be a CPA forever. He was missing a spark in this career for reasons he couldn't quite explain. He said to me, "I want something different to fill my cup."

Manny scored high on empathy and belief with StrengthsFinder. His childhood had been significantly impacted by his father dying from cancer when Manny was only seventeen. Now forty, Manny volunteered at the local AIDS hospice and raised money for Ronald McDonald House. We worked together to understand his skills and strengths, mapped them to appropriate positions, and assessed them across the domains of interpersonal, functional, and technical experiences. Through coaching and thoughtful self-reflection, Manny considered a career switch to nursing. After a few informational interviews, he quickly realized he wanted to stay in a more analytical role instead of moving to a front-line, patient-service role.

One networking call suggested Manny consider clinical trial work. This type of work is analytical in nature and helps new drugs get launched for the patients who need them. Manny investigated clinical-trial reporting positions that would leverage his skills and strengths in data, analysis, and detail-orientation and allow him to work in his passion industry. He prepared his personal branding messages and practiced interviewing. Today, Manny is a clinical trial operations lead, helping prepare the data analysis and reporting required to get new drug therapies approved for the patients who need them. He is working at the intersection of his skills, strengths, and core values.

So You're Thinking of Going Back to School?

If you've been thinking about going back to school, get serious about it. I'm that little voice on your shoulder saying, "Do it." At least, at a minimum, launch an earnest investigation.

My father dropped out of college. I didn't know that until I was thirty. He hid it from me because he was afraid of signaling that school wasn't important. He did go back and finish college in his fifties and continued on to a graduate degree to launch a new career in his passion area, the environment, at age fifty-five. He used an employer reimbursement program to finish school. My husband is perhaps one of the world's oldest PhD students right now as I type. He's gone back to school in his passion area, international relations, and has become a savvy Python coder. He discovered research grants to cover his tuition. Several friends have just finished, or are in pursuit of, their master's or PhD while juggling careers, relationships, and families.

Before you say, "It's too late," "It costs too much money," "I don't have time," or "What would I do with more schooling anyway?" do some research to make sure you aren't creating self-limiting beliefs. What evidence do you have that it's impossible to pursue your education goals? And remember, significant skills can be built using Coursera, LinkedIn, MasterClass, YouTube, and so many more democratized resources.

Staying fresh and relevant for the future you want for yourself may require more schooling. If going back to school is your itch, take action to scratch it.

Check out more tips for assessing your skills and strengths at www.the-me-suite.com/tools.

Combine this skills and strengths work with the primacy work you completed earlier for a powerful combination. If you know what your ideal role looks like and where your skills and strengths map to that ideal role, you'll be better able to prioritize the open positions you want to go after or create for yourself from scratch.

Physical and Mental Health: Control the Controllables

"You're fat," a director told me when I was a young adult pursuing my acting career. I wore a size twelve, and he wanted me to be a size six. I didn't develop eating disorders (no thanks to him), but I did become obsessed with the scale. Years later, as a consultant, I would yo-yo with my weight, given life on the road, eating restaurant food and room service. Honestly, I had spent so much time worrying about my weight as a rising actor earlier in my career that I resorted to a comfortable mindset of not caring about clothing sizes as my consulting career was rising. I decided clothing size didn't really matter—until it did.

I started testing as prediabetic in my early forties, and my triglycerides were treetop high. With the help of an expense account, I had eaten and imbibed myself toward metabolic syndrome at some of the finest establishments in the world. Sipping my signature gin and tonic on the back-porch glider one Friday at dusk, I watched a hummingbird coming for its sugar water in the feeder, and I let out a little "huh." I wasn't too different sitting here with my little sugar water, was I?

I thought about my core value of freedom, wanting to be free, not trapped. I thought about the limitations I'd have if my health continued on this path. I thought about how angry I'd be if something was in my control and I didn't do anything about it. Being healthier was in my control if I would just take control. I decided, there with the hummingbird as a witness, that it was time to make a change. I decided to vote on my priorities with my wallet and surround myself with personal training and nutrition experts for support. Surely, health coaches would be cheaper than diabetes care down the road, I calculated.

Quitting alcohol was the change that made the most positive impact on my overall health. My physical health, mental health, and the health of my relationship with my husband all improved when the alcohol evaporated from my life. While having no booze made the biggest difference, not drinking was the hardest change to manage socially for quite some time. It's hard to be the only one not drinking at a work function. I'd order a seltzer with lime and a swizzle stick to simulate a gin and tonic. This helped deter any questions until someone returned with a second round. It's hard when you say, "I'll have water," and the colleague replies, while pouring, "Oh you've got to try this cab. It is so good. Just a sip. Come on."

I've been asked if I was pregnant. I've been asked if I'd gotten a DUI. Couldn't it simply be that I didn't want alcohol? Fast forward to today, and I just say it straight with no chaser. "I don't drink booze, but I'd love a seltzer with a lime." I am no longer prediabetic, and my triglycerides are gorgeous. I work to keep it that way every day. (I can also deadlift 185 pounds—personal best is twenty-one times consecutively—in case you need any help moving some furniture.)

The healthier you are, the more options you have. It's that simple. Summarizing Aristotle, philosopher Will Durant wrote, "We are what we repeatedly do."[25] There is so much you cannot control about your mental and physical health, so you must control the controllables by repeatedly doing the right things with intention. I'm talking about the need to keep a healthy mind and body, focusing more on vital signs and quality of life than on clothing sizes. On the physical dimension, health means knowing your numbers, starting with the basic bloodwork panel: blood pressure, cholesterol, A1C, triglycerides, thyroid, C-reactive protein, and other relevant metrics.

If you think you don't have time to go to the doctor now, imagine where you'll find the four hours a day the average adult diabetic needs

---

[25] Frank Heron, "It's a Much More Effective Quotation to Attribute It to Aristotle, Rather Than to Will Durant," The Art of Quotemanship and Misquotemanship, October 3, 2021, https://blogs.umb.edu/quoteunquote/2012/05/08/its-a-much-more-effective-quotation-to-attribute-it-to-aristotle-rather-than-to-will-durant/#:~:text=After%20quoting%20a%20phrase%20from,quotes%20again%20from%20Aristotle's%20work.

to manage the disease.[26] Complete the recommended diagnostics for your age range and family history on schedule, and listen to your body. Don't ignore small problems and changes. A recent RAND study showed a 14% increase in drinking among those over thirty and a 41% increase in heavy drinking among women during the pandemic. As you return to more work and social environments, advocate for what you need to be in control of your health.[27]

Certified Personal Trainer Jason Rumpf[28] and I partnered to create the SEESAW model as a simple tool for keeping your health in balance.

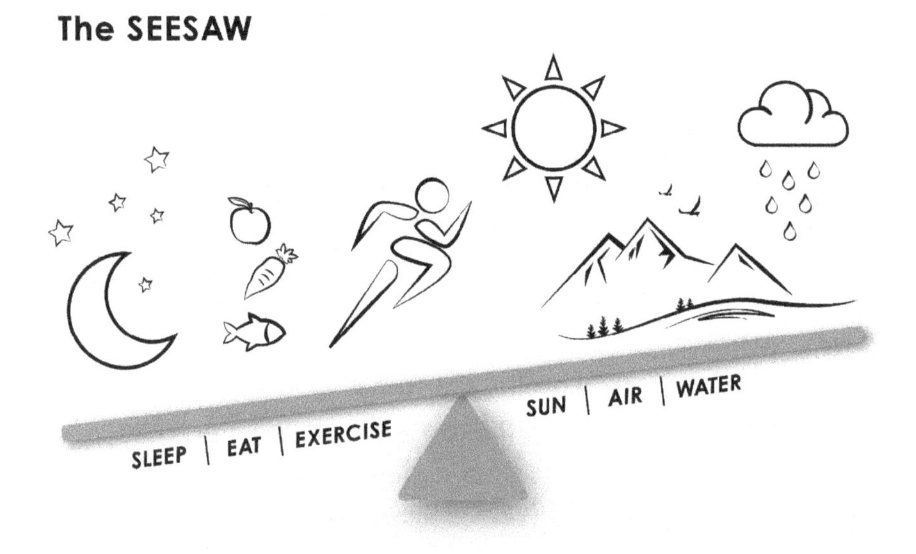

[26] Jay H. Shubrook, et al., "Time Needed for Diabetes Self-Care: Nationwide Survey of Certified Diabetes Educators," American Diabetes Association, August 31, 2018, https://spectrum.diabetesjournals.org/content/31/3/267.
[27] Michael S. Pollard, "Alcohol Consumption Rises Sharply During Pandemic Shutdowm," RAND Corporation, September 29, 2020. https://www.rand.org/news/press/2020/09/29.html.
[28] Jason Rumpf, Atlanta's Top Trainer, October 3, 2021, https://www.atltoptrainer.com/.

The SEESAW elements are:

- Sleep. Get good, quality sleep, consistently.
- Eat. Consume clean, unprocessed foods. I leaned on *Performing Nutrition*[29] and *Healthy Weight Coaching*[30] to build the right behaviors and make the best decisions. My previous lack of nutrition education still amazes me. It's not just about calories.
- Exercise. Include these five priority movements during each exercise session: 1) upper body push, 2) upper body pull, 3) squatting, 4) hinging at the hip, and 5) core stabilization.
- Sun. Get some vitamin D and serotonin uptake to boost your mood.[31]
- Air. Breathe deeply. Oxygen intake and cortisol reduction lower stress.
- Water. Hydration is simple and has a multitude of health benefits.

The SEESAW elements all serve your mental and your physical well-being, but SEESAW alone is not enough at times. Like many of you, I am a career-driven professional whose family has walked a minefield of depression, addiction, anxiety, and suicide.

Here's what that minefield has looked like for me:

- I've answered my cell at 2:00 a.m., far away in a random Marriott hotel, to hear a relative tell me she had a gun and planned to use it.
- I've installed a locking mailbox after my identity was stolen by an addict I was trying to help.
- I've stepped out of a client meeting to tell the police, "Yes, launch the search and rescue team to find him."

---

[29] https://www.performingnutrition.com/.

[30] https://healthyweightcoaching.com/.

[31] Amberlee Lovell Peterson, "7 Health Benefits of Sunlight," Select Health, October 3, 2021, https://selecthealth.org/blog/2020/07/7-health-benefits-of-sunlight.

- I've spent weekends visiting the ER more times than I can remember.
- I've fabricated answers to: "So sorry. He was so young. How did ___ die?"
- I know the panic when the phone rings and rings and no one picks up.
- I've attended the overdose funerals and the suicide funeral.

Most people on the outside looking in would not suspect my personal life had been so touched by mental health needs. I hid it pretty well. I don't hide it anymore, and I frequently remind my coaching clients that leadership and high performance at any level, at any title, can be a lonely position. Advocate for what you need, and be an advocate for others. Channel your inner Simone Biles and Naomi Osaka. Meditation, mindfulness, yoga, nature walks, face-to-face social connection, and positive words are all proven to positively impact mental health.[32] I mentioned earlier that we are awake working and doing activities related to work more hours than we are awake and doing nothing related to work. Mind your mind.

Forming habits is critical here. Find what works for you. For example, I spent a lot of time and money believing I had to love yoga. *Everyone loves yoga. Why am I not loving yoga? What's wrong with me for not loving yoga? Maybe if I keep trying, I'll learn to love yoga like an arranged fitness marriage.* At first, the words "calming" and "peaceful" filled my head with anticipation. I even went out and bought my own mat, knowing I'd get addicted to yoga right away. I was surprised the mat was so cheap. Turns out, by mistake, I bought a foam cushion made to be used with a sleeping bag when you go camping.

After too many attempts to count, I finally developed the confidence to admit out loud that yoga is a "no-ga" for me. No more

[32] CBHS Health, "What is positive mental health and how can we foster it?" August 17, 2021, https://www.cbhs.com.au/mind-and-body/blog/what-is-positive-mental-health-and-how-can-we-foster-it.

stretching strangers passing gas all around me. No more mat neighbors snoring through my shavasana. My version of meditation and mindfulness is gardening. Find what fits you best, and embed it in your daily rhythm. The quality of your options is directly correlated with the status of your physical and mental health.

Finances: Make Informed, Planful Decisions About Money

When my husband came back from a Miami fishing trip we couldn't afford, proudly hauling his six-foot, taxidermic barracuda, financed at 21% APR, I was apoplectic. There was no active listening. "What did you do?" I yelled. There was no appreciative inquiry. I was vein-popping mad. By the time the fish was paid off, it cost about $600 in real money and about $2,000 in relationship currency. The beast hangs on display to this day as a reminder of the first impressionable "money moment that mattered" in our relationship.

There's also the money moment with the star that topped our first Christmas tree. We cut it from a manila folder and wrapped it in aluminum foil. Every year we pull it out of the ornament box, straighten the curled edges, and laugh about rolling loose change on the den floor that winter. That $78 in coins bought a lot of groceries.

My husband, Jonathan, and I both grew up in family businesses, so we were used to financial conversations happening openly, not always pleasantly, around us. Talking about money was normal. It was necessary and literally in the family DNA. This may be the risk-taking gene that led us to start a business together in our mid-twenties while still dating. Our business was corporate catering and a lunch-only restaurant. Jonathan was the chef—and a darn good one—and I ran the operations when not out on acting auditions.

Our first year in business, while living in my future mother-in-law's basement, I qualified for the earned income tax credit, a level of broke that is almost impossible to achieve without children. I paid off credit card A with credit card B. We argued over Jonathan joining a book-of-the-month club. It seemed pathetic to start a fight because my boyfriend wanted to read more literature, but every book seemed like another month I'd be in that basement. I missed a dear friend's wedding because I couldn't afford the flight and hotel room. Broke, broke, broke.

That level of broke led us to our most enduring money moment that mattered, the social contract. It exists to this day. Young and broke, Jonathan and I committed to not spend over $200 without consulting the other person first. A $200 limit practically covered a typical grocery shopping trip and a common ATM visit, and it put reins on random purchases like electronics and clothing. But really, we did it because the $200 threshold kept us from overdrawing the checking account when the left wallet didn't know what the right wallet was doing. Over twenty-five years later, we still have this social contract in place. The threshold has an extra zero in it, but the principles still apply and help us keep a unified front toward the financial goals that fuel our options.

"You're never powerful in life until you're powerful over your own money." ~ *Suze Orman*

Money matters because it plays a necessary role in your ability to do what you want, when you want, with whom you want. Money can fuel or extinguish your options. Consider five practices when it comes to the role finances play in building your options.

First, The Social Contract: If you're in a committed relationship, have an agreement about the amount of money you can each spend without alerting the other person. If you find receipts are being hidden or private accounts are being opened, you don't have a unified front toward your goals.

Second, The Spreadsheet: Maintain a spreadsheet that calculates the impact of saving versus spending. This forces a long-term mindset, which is different from the weekly or monthly budget management. Use the spreadsheet (or a similar tool) to jointly assess the impact of your larger financial decisions. For example, if purchasing Car A over Car B saves $20,000, where could that extra $20,000 best be applied to your goals? If you stay in your current smaller home another five years, how much closer to retirement could you be, and do you care? Is the $50,000 in unvested stock worth staying at that stressful job for another year? If one of you has just lost a job or needs to walk away from a job, how will the loss of income be absorbed? The spreadsheet gives you a quick read on the long-term impact of real-time decisions. You may still decide to make the big expenditure or leave the higher-paying job, but you'll do so with two (or four) eyes wide open.

Third, The Gift Shift: Use The Social Contract and The Spreadsheet to shift your mindset about giving and receiving gifts. What financial boundaries do you want to place on gifting based on your financial goals? I've read Gary Chapman's *The 5 Love Languages.*[33] I understand some couples want the element of surprise with gift-giving. I'm not a complete and total buzzkill, but I believe gifting should respect the Social Contract and honor the Spreadsheet. Be intentional.

For example, a savvy way to boost your gift fund is to use a cash-back credit card for all household purchases. Put all groceries, supplies, and gas on the same card, and pay in full monthly. At the end of the year, take the

---

[33] Gary Chapman, *The 5 Love Languages* (Chicago: Northfield Publishing, 2015).

accumulated reward points as your gift fund. It'll feel like finding free money.

Fourth, Total Cost of Ownership: Train your brain to consider the total cost of ownership of your larger purchases, such as housing, transportation, and education. A house is not just a mortgage payment. It also comes with interest, insurance, maintenance, furnishings, utilities, taxes, fees, and tax deductions. I was raised to believe renting was throwing money down the drain. If you study the work of Nobel Prize-winning economist, Robert Shiller, you'll have your traditional assumptions about home ownership truly challenged. His research shows the many ways in which home ownership may not be the wisest decision if you consider the data and the options.[34] The point is to make an informed decision, and consult financial experts as needed.

Fifth, Being More Swedish: This topic may be uncomfortable, but it's exactly the discomfort we need to discuss—the one thing that unites us all—regardless of sex, race, religion, socioeconomic status, education, geography, how we love. Everybody dies. Be more open, realistic, and prepared.

Over the last few years, I have settled three estates. One estate, my father's, was well-planned throughout an illness. My father talked me through a list of fifty-seven items I was to execute for my mother after he passed. And it was difficult. The second estate involved two complicated trusts with ancient documentation in a dysfunctional family, and it was difficult. The third was a suicide with no will, and it was difficult. It's always difficult.

With a Me-Suite mindset, I'm reminded to practice specific actions to remain grounded in the now and confidently plan for the inevitable. Show gratitude. Think about the person you've been meaning to thank, and thank them this week. It will feel so good.

---

[34] Greg Rosalsky, "Is Buying a Home Overrated?" Planet Money, April 30, 2019, https://www.npr.org/sections/money/2019/04/30/718348115/is-buying-a-house-overrated.

"Let each thing you would do, say, or intend, be like that of a dying person." ~ *Marcus Aurelius*

Adopt *dostadning* (no, this is not a typo). Acknowledge that we are not here forever and we don't know our final day. Have open conversations about the one thing that binds us all—the fact that life is never long enough. And yes, this can be very awkward at all ages. Check out the book *The Gentle Art of Swedish Death Cleaning: How to Free Yourself and Your Family from a Lifetime of Clutter.*

Have the right papers. Consult an estate-planning attorney, no matter your age. At a minimum, we all need a will, a durable power of attorney, a healthcare directive, and insurance documentation. We also need a list of account numbers, passwords, key contacts, and locations of safes or storage facilities. More complicated affairs may require trusts and additional powers of attorney. Having financial options is not about making the most money. It's about making the most informed decisions about money.

These decisions include:

- Employment
    - What makes a job "worth it" to me?
    - What benefits does my employer offer, and which of those benefits should I use?
    - What do I need to consider if I'm self-employed?
    - Should I go back to school?
- Family
    - How do I want to plan for /support a family (single, partnered, married, divorced, kids)?
    - How will college be funded for the kids?
    - Will I inherit anything?
    - What inheritance do I want to leave for others?

- Home ownership
    - What is the total cost of owning a home?
    - Should I purchase or rent?
- Retirement
    - When do I plan to retire, and what does being retired mean to me?
    - How much money will I need in retirement?
    - How much should I be saving?
    - How should I be investing?
- Advice
    - Do I need a financial planner? Commission-based or fee-only?
    - Do I really understand taxes? As Otis Aust of Aust Financial Advisory says on *The Me-Suite* podcast, season 1, episode 19, "At age eighteen, you'll be in a relationship with the Internal Revenue Service for the rest of your life."
    - What role will charitable contributions play in the allocation of my time and money?
    - What legal documents do I need in place and kept current?

Now, take every I, me, and my in the questions above, and replace them with the even more stress-inducing we, us, and our. If you're in a relationship, these decisions become we, us, our decisions. Not surprisingly, *Psychology Today* research indicates financial stressors cause relationship quality to suffer because people tend to resort to negative communication patterns in difficult financial circumstances[35]. The 2021

[35] Susan Krauss Whitbourne, "Is Your Relationship Suffering From Money Problems?" *Psychology Today*, November 28, 2020, https://www.psychologytoday.com/us/blog/fulfillment-any-age/202011/is-your-relationship-suffering-money-problems.

Fidelity Investments Couples and Money Study found one in five couples identified money as their greatest relationship challenge[36].

Interestingly, of the six most common money matters couples discuss, the topic of careers ranked the most difficult.

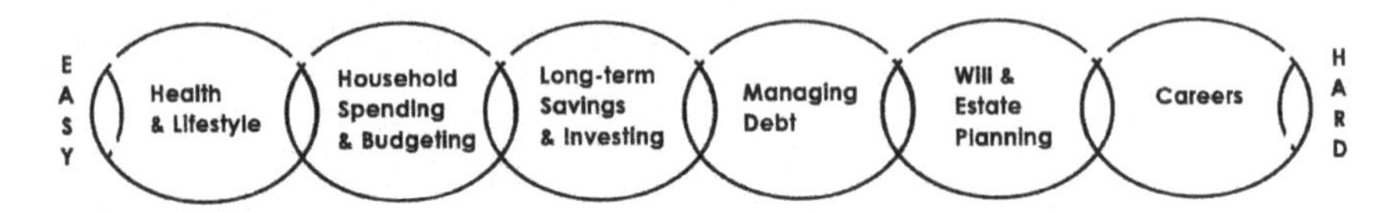

The Fidelity study also showed that the 2020-2021 COVID-19 pandemic increased the financial stress for Millennial and Gen-X couples by about 40%, with 51% disagreeing on the amount of savings they needed to retire and 48% disagreeing on the age they plan to retire. Look your finances in the face if you want options.

Teach Your Pet Budgeting Skills

Pets have played a feature role in many of our COVID lives. When I saw the "pet" slice in my 2020-2021 spending pie chart, however, I passed out. When I came to and dug into the data, I saw how my cats had so thoughtfully distributed their expenditures over the year. In the spring, Kenny required multiple compound-pharmacy medicines for his various organ maladies.

By summer, Dubbie had developed a nasal stricture that required emergency surgery. Perhaps a clinic wing will be named for him following that little excursion. And Lil' Girl developed a mysterious bump on her head in the winter that remains undiagnosed and under surveillance. Whoever said mutt animals are healthier than pure breeds is delusional. I recommend opening a PSA, a pet savings account, or just investing in becoming a vet. The school loans may come out a little cheaper, or at a minimum, you'll likely break even.

---

[36] Fidelity Investments, "2021 Couples & Money Study," https://www.fidelity.com/bin-public/060_www_fidelity_com/documents/about-fidelity/Fidelity-Couples-and-Money-Fact-Sheet-2021.pdf.

What Is Your Re-tirement Plan?

When I left my corporate leadership position at Accenture in 2020 after eighteen-plus years, I described my move as re-tiring, as in getting new tires. There's the FIRE movement—financially independent, retire early. We have the gig economy of contractors. Ninety-one percent of millennials expect to change jobs every three years. We have the Great Resignation fueled by the pandemic. All these career trends have common themes. We all age, we need to plan for the life we want to live when we're older, and we need to be realistic about the role money plays in that plan.

"Why are we vaccinating old people since they'll die anyway?" "The world would be better if the older people just died off." These are real quotes I heard in conversations during the pandemic. Our society has a toxic religion of "retire at sixty-five," an engineered concept that is partly to blame for the age-old bias against birthdays. In 1880, Germany was the first country to set the retirement age at sixty-five, a convenient age for introducing social security since few people were expected to live that long. The U.S. retirement age of sixty-five was set in 1935, for similar actuarial reasons, when the average lifespan was only sixty-two years.[37] Thanks to science and innovation, today the average U.S. lifespan is seventy-nine years, ranking #46 among the world's countries. (Hong Kong and Japan have the highest at eighty-five.)[38]

It's helpful to reset your mindset on what retirement could entail for you by considering some inspirational facts. In 2021, the U.S. president was 78; the head of treasury, 74; the secretary of defense, 67; the Speaker of the House, 80. Five Supreme Court justices were 65 or older; the Dalai Lama, 85; and poet and Presidential Medal of

---

[37] Sarah Ovaska-Few, "How 65 Became the Retirement Age," *Journal of Accountancy*, March 1, 2018, https://www.journalofaccountancy.com/issues/2018/mar/how-65-became-default-retirement-age.html.
[38] "Life Expectancy of the World Population 2021", Worldometer, https://www.worldometers.info/demographics/life-expectancy/.

Freedom honoree Suzan Harjo, 75. Actor and dancer Rita Moreno was 89, as was Dan Rather (I hang on his every tweet). Congressman John Lewis served until his death at age 80. Maya Angelou wrote and inspired the world until age 86. Ruth Bader Ginsburg heard cases until her passing at age 87. Imagine a world where contributions from these genius talents were severed at age 65. On second thought, don't imagine that because it's a terrible image.

Think about it this way. At age sixty-five, you'll live about fifteen more years based on life expectancy statistics. Whatever your age today, look at all you've accomplished and experienced in your various fifteen-year spurts. From age 15 to 30, 20 to 35, 35 to 50, 40 to 55, 45 to 60, 50 to 65, and beyond.

If you retire early, what will you do with 50 to 80? If you take the traditional retirement path, what will you do with 65 to 80? What will you need to be fresh and relevant through that time?

Think about adding these questions to your personal strategic planning at every age:

- Is there someone 65+ today who I want to be like when I'm their age?
- What lifestyle will I be living at 65? What will be a "day in the life" for me?
- How will I define retirement, resting or re-tiring (as in getting new tires for a fresh road ahead)?
- What am I doing now to set myself up for my definition of retirement? Planning financially, refreshing my skills, nurturing passions, prioritizing wellness, keeping friendships warm?

If doing absolutely nothing with those fifteen years is your thing, then name it and enjoy it, but be planful so you have options.

CHOOSE HOW YOU SHOW UP

One of my favorite parts of keynote speaking is the Q&A session. This is my chance to determine if my concepts hit home with the audience and how well they absorbed my intended messages, or not. At one such conference on leadership, I was asked, "What do good leaders do?"

First, I clarified the question with a question. "Do you mean people with a leadership title on an org chart or people with a leadership mindset?" Leadership, after all, is a mindset. Thousands of books, research projects, classes, podcasts, and pundits surround us with perspectives on leadership. All the work is thoughtful, but often the insights are a parade of synonyms and platitudes. The term "leader" is often associated with vision-setter, decision-maker, prioritizer, motivator, delegator, communicator, listener, problem-solver, or challenger.

Good leaders simply do two things. They sense and signal. Sensing is the leadership antenna that *absorbs* information. Sensing leaders stay tuned in to the frequency of customers, competitors, employees, market trends, technology developments, and environmental shifts. They question, assuming positive intent. They listen, seeking to understand. In short, they sense with empathy.

Empathy: The New Leadership Currency

Empathy is the essence of our era. We take personality assessments that rank our empathy tendencies. We attend training to recognize the biases that make us less empathetic. We deploy design-thinking techniques to empathize with the user experience. These are important and necessary. At the same time, we tend to talk about empathy as something outside of ourselves that we're trying to find and bring inside.

Empathy is already within you. Empathy is what makes you love your favorite character in a movie. Empathy is what draws you into a book you can't put down. Empathy is what moves you to call a laid-off colleague, hug a crying baby, celebrate a friend's promotion.

Actors are perhaps the best empathizers because they must seek to understand the other without judging. Actors specialize in putting themselves in others' shoes, understanding a situation from another's point of view even when it's the opposite of their own views. When it comes to the empathy muscle, actors are professional bodybuilders.

You can train your empathy muscle like an actor by asking:

1. Why does that person see the situation the way they do? How can I honor their perspective?
2. What is the other person's motivation? What do they want, and why?
3. If I were in their shoes, how would I be thinking differently?

As leaders, we all get pretty good at socializing ideas, pressure-testing recommendations, doing a little *nemawashi* (the meeting before the meeting) to manage stakeholders. These actions can be a bit manipulative if we have only our own agenda at play. Prepare like an actor. Get into the head of the other "characters" with these three questions to amp up empathy.

Signaling is the leadership antenna that shares information. Leaders who signal consistently emit the company's core values, vision, expectations, and tone. They are accessible (like a strong human Wi-Fi connection) and communicate with intention. They signal their trust through strategic engagement and delegation.

Think about a leader you find particularly effective. What are examples of how they sense and signal? The next time you walk into a room, join a video call, text, or send an email, how will you sense and signal as a leader? If you're sensing and signaling, you're in the fabric, knitting together options for the company's next best moves.

Who Are You as a Leader, and Why?

"As leaders, we interpret and respond to situations as if scenes from our family history."[39] ~*Dr. Marjorie Blum*

For the last three years, I've studied how family inheritances impact leadership styles. There is nothing about your life—including how you show up at work—that your family experiences do not impact, both genetically and psychologically. From the way you were raised to argue and give praise to the multigenerational stories you grew up telling or not telling. You see this play out weekly on *Finding Your Roots,* where Dr. Henry Louis Gates Jr. helps write a chapter in each guest's book of "Who am I?"

Inspired by the work of Dr. Blum and Dr. Gates, I headed out on a road trip with my mom, Flo, in tow. My goal was to live some family history in South Alabama and gain more insights into how family inheritances have shaped my leadership style. If you're a follower of my blog, you know I "Go with the Flo" frequently and the moments never disappoint. We've traveled to ten countries together with only one threat of arrest when Flo crossed the security barrier to touch Napoleon's drapery at Fontainebleau and guards rushed out from behind the mahogany paneling like startled mice in berets.

The narrow country back roads of South Alabama were largely well maintained, but the shoulders were dangerously deep from years

[39] "Why We Act the Way We Do at Work," The Me-Suite Podcast Season 3, Episode 16, May 13, 2021.

of layering asphalt over asphalt. The lanes were super straight through loamy land, until they weren't. Random right-angle curves, punctuated by an abandoned general store, appeared like a mirage. The lonely passages were hooded by the greenest green oaks and poplars, almost a lime green at the cusp of summer. The churches seemed to be placed accidentally on purpose in a zigzag pattern bouncing from the left side of the road to the right side, and I commented, "There are more churches around here than people." Tiny graveyards seemed as frequent as cattle sprinkled off the sides of the road. While the headstones were weathered, the fresh flowers indicated recent respect.

We weren't completely sure where we were going, but we knew the town was called Sprott, and the landmark we needed was a church on a hill with a graveyard, a church called Mount Something. This area was pretty flat, so if we investigated the few hilly parts, we were likely to find our gravesite. The side roads off the main county strip were either unnamed or named after people. Not the usual Roosevelt Road or Smithfield Street, but literally named after the people who lived at the end of that very road.

We took a narrow, unnamed lane headed straight up the steep mountain like a rollercoaster track. I was driving faster than I should, surprised at how excited I was for this adventure. Finally, we arrived at Mount Pleasant Church graveyard. We walked through the chain-link gate as if entering a ball field, more waddling than walking because we were a little stiff from so much sitting on the long drive. The Taylor family plots were immediately off to the right. There were so many of them, lined up like a family photo from biggest to smallest.

From left to right, the concrete roll call started with the humble laborers, Hosea and Amanda (my great-grandparents), followed by six of their twelve children. The children cascaded from fifteen years old down to an infant. Two of the children were buried together after drowning in the river. One's dress caught fire. One had a tumor. We weren't sure of the gruesome reason the two others died so young. Another six children survived to adulthood and went on to raise their own families. One was my grandfather. He left school in the eighth grade to work on the railroad and help support the family, retiring after fifty years of service. He had eight children of his own, losing the eldest at twelve months old. Mom was number seven and the only surviving girl. She reminded me that much of the rail her daddy laid had now been ripped up or abandoned, invisible under kudzu. She seemed a little saddened by that thought.

Genetically and psychologically, this is part of who I am and how I show up as a leader. Through this simple road trip experience, and I hope many others, I'm growing to understand what it means to bring my whole self to work. I'm getting more comfortable sharing my own story and encouraging others to share theirs. Everyone has a family of some definition. Study your family inheritances to understand who you are as a leader, and recognize the power and influence that other people's family inheritances have on how they show up.

Delegate Is Delegrow

Delegation is the most common performance challenge I see in my executive coaching practice. High performers who want to take on greater responsibility are the very ones struggling to delegate work that would free up time for them to do so. It's a common leadership paradox, but a simple mindset shift will help you work through it. I call it "delegrow."

When you've received feedback, you may have heard:

- You need to focus on more strategic issues.
- Why do you send emails so late at night and on the weekends?
- I'd like to engage you in this new important initiative, but you have so much on your plate.

Simultaneously, you may be saying to yourself:

- It's just faster if I do it myself.
- I don't want to dump this task on her.
- He's got a lot going on already.

It is impossible—absolutely impossible—for you to develop others if you do not delegate work that allows them to grow. Conversely, it is impossible—absolutely impossible—for you to develop yourself if you are not delegated work that allows you to grow. But how can you take on more without giving more to others?

Delegation doesn't mean "shove this off on someone else." Delegation means "appoint as my representative." As a leader, you are probably afraid that you'll be seen as the bad boss dumping busy work on already busy people. Or you, yourself, are so busy it's a waste of time to stop and involve others. This faulty thinking works against your very goals to grow others and grow yourself.

When you adopt the mindset of "delegrow," you will ask different questions, such as:

- What activities could I assign my team to build their skills and their knowledge?
- What activities could I assign my team to build their networks and their sense of ownership?
- What activities should I be seeking to grow myself?

Yes, brown stuff does roll downhill sometimes. The truth is not all work is strategic and sexy. Tedious, crappy assignments exist at all levels, but what might be crappy data clean-up work to you could be an opportunity for someone else to learn the company's chart of accounts. What might be mind-numbing slide editing to you was a chance for me to hone executive presentation skills, and I was even happy doing it on a Sunday because I got exposure to the leadership team at their offsite.

You need a mindset that growth—your personal growth and your ability to grow others—requires delegation. The more you delegate, the more options come available to you and to others because the intention for both parties is growth. Tomorrow, think about what delegated task you'll ask to take on from someone else and what you will delegate.

360-Degree Feedback That Made Me Do a 180

Have you ever had 360-degree feedback that made you do a 180? I used to think I was being supportive. I'd encourage my team members to take their PTO by saying, "No one is so important they can't take PTO." Then, I got my 360 feedback results. Someone had taken the time to write a thoughtful, constructive comment.

"Donna says no one is so important they can't take PTO. I find this demotivating. I wish she instead would say that I am important, but not all the time."

Wow. That feedback has stuck with me for over fifteen years. I learned through sensing that, at work, you're important, but not all the time. At home, you're important all the time. I now try to signal that to those in my sphere.

The 3-Way Stop and Think

Stop and think about these three ways to shape how you show up: First is your impression and body language. What is the impression you want to leave? How is that aligned to your core values and how you want to show up? How will you enter the room? Will you sit or stand, in the front or the back? Will you be texting under the table? What will you wear? If remote, how will you use the video camera?

Next is your intentions and tone. When actors are studying a character, they study the intentions of the character to understand why that character thinks as he does, why she made a decision, why the characters react as they do. Your actions follow your intentions. Your intention comes first. If your intention is to humiliate someone, feedback will come out of your mouth very differently than if your true intention is to help someone improve. Think about this the next time you're fussing with your partner or arguing with the bank over the phone. What are your true intentions in that interaction?

Last is simple and clear words. Your goal when you communicate should be to be understood. That doesn't mean the other person will agree, but understanding should be your goal. A great tool for practicing simple and clear communications is the trick of the haiku. I call it the MyKu. The haiku is a Japanese poetry form requiring three lines of five, seven, and five syllables, respectively. It's a great tool to force clarity and focus on the real point you're trying to make. And why use thirty lines when three will suffice? As Mark Twain is attributed to have written, "I apologize for such a long letter. I didn't have time to write a short one." Example MyKus include:

I want a refund.
Amazon delivered late.
Can you help me please?

Wonderful event.
Do I owe you anything?
Let me pay my part.

This is not working.
You need to pull your own weight.
Let's sit down and chat.

How to Say "More Chocolate Please" in Any Language

Communications research has shown that body language is more influential than words or tone. Some research indicates body language is roughly sixty percent of a communication.[40] The needed balance of words, tone, and body language can change significantly, for example, with digital platforms and remote working, but the three components of communications remain and must be deliberately managed.[41]

There is a universal language for "More chocolate, please." While I was in Switzerland several years ago for work, a woman came to my hotel room to replenish the cups. We had a thorough, delightful communication. Although my verbal language was gibberish to her and hers was gibberish to me, our body language—smiles, gestures, open posture—were clear and inviting.

Without communicating with words, I fully understood she was sorry to have forgotten the cups when she came by earlier, and she was asking with wide eyes, "May I drop these off right now, and would you like some more Toblerone?" I had eaten the entire bowl of Toblerone since she came by that morning. The wrappers were scattered about, so I had to confess I did eat them all, right then and there. And yes, please, I'd like some more.

---

[40] Dustin, Smith, Lifesize, "Nonverbal Communication," https://www.lifesize.com/en/blog/speaking-without-words/, February 18, 2020.
[41] Philip Yaffe "The 7% Rule. Fact, Fiction and Misunderstanding," Ubiquity, Volume 2011, issue October, October 2011, https://ubiquity.acm.org/article.cfm?id=2043156.

Make Every Word Count

The most common feedback I hear when I conduct 360-degree feedback interviews on behalf of clients is "This person talks too much." This can mean they don't get to the point quickly enough, or their thoughts are scattered, or they aren't effective in the stories they tell. The context may be situational, but the feedback is the same. Fundamentally, the leader is not communicating clearly. The leader is using fifty words when fifteen would have sufficed. The leader is rambling. The leader's point isn't clear.

In my twenty-plus years working with senior leaders, I know an inverse relationship exists between the individual's seniority and the number of words they use. More senior is fewer words, fewer slides, less time. Leaders are precise. Leaders are clear. Leaders have little time. We all have little time.

In the 1800s, sending a telegram was a precious experience both for the sender and the recipient. Every word counted, literally.

A ten-word message in today's dollars costs:

- New York to New Orleans - $75
- New York to Los Angeles - $200
- New York to London - $2,600

Today, our words don't count, not literally anyway. We can talk forever on the phone or virtually for a flat fee. We have unlimited text. Even though Twitter limits the character count to 280 (up from its original 140), the cost is carried by the provider, so we tweet away. In the twenty-first century, we are incented to go on and on. If our words literally counted, we'd be much more intentional and thoughtful in our communications. Give it a try. The next time you need to get to the core of your big message, imagine you had only $200 for the telegram. In ten words, what would that telegram say? That, my friend, is your core message. You may even decide to save a little money and make it only five words. Victor Hugo, author of *The Hunchback of Notre Dame*, was said to have sent the shortest-ever telegram inquiring how the launch of his new book, *Les Miserables*, was being received.

Hugo's telegram: "?"

Publisher's response: "!"

Business Theatre

You can be the smartest person in the room with the most insightful ideas, but if you can't communicate in a way that engages people to think differently or take action, you haven't really made an impact.

Business is where people work together
to make or sell a product or service.
+
Theatre is a form of storytelling
that uses engagement
to create an experience.
=
Business Theatre is
intentional leadership impact.

In every moment of business, you are creating a shared experience, sometimes intentionally, most often a bit mindlessly, as you go about your day, checking off boxes and getting things done. For example, if you join a Zoom call late and others have been waiting on you, there are a few options.

Your options include:

The Center of the Universe. You join late and waste even more time explaining the details of why you're late. "My call with client X ran over." "I ran into the SVP, and needed to catch her while I had the time." Here, you project that you're late because the prior engagement was more important than all those who joined on time or you didn't respect the impact your poor planning has on others. Here, the subconscious intention is to show you had no choice but to be late, and you continue to waste time with the dramatic details.

The Hijacker. You join hurried and may be a little flustered since you've been running behind all day. You hijack the team vibe with your rushed frustration. Here, the subconscious intention is to let off steam by venting a little about how busy you are. As if no one else is as busy.

The Leader. You apologize, genuinely, for wasting people's time, acknowledge everyone present with a simple greeting, confirm the meeting will end at the planned time, and get to the task at hand. Here, the goal is intentional—to acknowledge the impact your lateness has on others and use the remaining time respectfully and productively. The third option requires intention—being intentional about the experience you want to create in the business moment. It requires that you are thoughtful about the desired experience, as a director would be in staging a play, and then perform that intention.

Think about these moments in business:

- Presenting a big proposal
- Hosting a town hall meeting
- Conducting a workshop to create next year's business plan
- Job interviewing
- Meeting someone for the first time
- Giving or receiving feedback
- Leading or attending a Zoom meeting

These examples vary by degree of formality, by internal or external audiences, by how high you perceive the stakes to be in that moment. What they all have in common is that you will make an impact in each of these scenarios—but are you making the impact you intend? Your magic as a leader is in creating the experience you intentionally want to share, and the best place to turn for lessons in creating experiences is the theatre.

I have a Master of Fine Arts in acting, a three-year terminal degree. Terminal sounds like it's fatal, and I guess in some ways it is fatal if you consider that about 90% of actors are out of work at any given time.[42] In addition, resilience, complete surrender to feedback, and fortress-thick skin are required to complete such a program, so when you graduate, you really feel as if you've survived something. Terminal here actually means it's the highest degree achievable in its field. From the theatre field of study and acting for ten years, I learned all that goes into creating the audience engagement and shared moments of a theatre experience. Every day, I bring that knowledge to my corporate work. I'm passionate about leaders bringing the disciplines of theatre into business to improve impact.

Consider the theatre components and how they show up in the business environment. The major disciplines that come together in a theatrical production to create a shared experience are director, script, cast, audience, set design, costumes, lighting, sound, and props.

Here's how these disciplines apply to business meetings:

- Director: the sponsor of the meeting; the person who has decided why this meeting, why now.
- Script: the key messages to be conveyed during the meeting.
- Cast: the people presenting, sharing the key messages.
- Audience: the people who need to absorb the key messages.
- Set, Lighting, and Sound: the vibe, the tone you want to establish with the physical or virtual space.
- Costumes: the dress code.
- Props: the materials required.

---

[42] Michael Simkins, "Only 2% of Actors Make a Living," *The Guardian*, June 5, 2019, https://www.theguardian.com/film/shortcuts/2019/jun/05/only-2-per-cent-of-actors-make-a-living-how-do-you-become-one-of-them.

With a business-theatre mindset, you become intentional about the experience being created. Small things make a big difference in creating that desired experience. Here's how this plays out in a high-stakes interaction, in this case, a sales presentation to win work with a client.

The director, the sponsor of the meeting, decides why this meeting and why now. The sales lead and the client counterpart are co-directors in this instance. They align on the desired outcomes of the meeting and the general format. The sales lead rehearses the lines and blocking (where to stand and when and where to move) with the sales team.

For the script, the sales lead "writes the script," outlining the key messages that need to land. This also includes which "cast member" says which lines and when. If we're running behind, what's the catch-up plan?

With the cast, what team members are required to deliver the messages that create the desired outcome? Considering the audience, the sales lead and client counterpart align on who is joining from the client side. Are they all in person, remote, hybrid? How will you greet each audience member at the start?

For the set, lighting, and sound, the sales lead requests whatever is necessary to create the desired physical or virtual environment. What is the room setup? Where will salespeople and clients sit? How will catering be brought in? If virtual, does the sales team all use the same background? What if a team member loses connectivity? Do you want the sales team sitting interspersed with the clients or sitting off to the side?

The costumes matter more than you realize. Should the sales team be dressed the same to show unity? Will the team be dressed slightly more formally than the audience? Same as the audience? The props are the materials required. Will PowerPoint be presented? Printed? Pre-read? Are there other materials needed to help facilitate breakouts or interactivity? Do you share the slides one by one so people can't read ahead? What if some audience members are in person and others remote? How will you disperse materials?

I experienced a colleague mastering business theatre to win a significant contract with a client. His intentional attention to business-theatre details created a shared experience and ultimate win. The sales lead and client lead co-presented at the top of the meeting to signal alignment. The sales team had practiced their lines and movement like a play rehearsal. Each team member knew how and when transitions from one person to the next would occur. Each knew how they'd use the room. Each knew when the printouts would be shared and who would take notes on the flip chart. Each knew what to add if a team member forgot to stress a key point.

The sales team sat mingled among the client audience and each had a client "match" they were to build rapport with during the meeting. The sales team had decided how they wanted to engage with the different client players to help build rapport at the start of the meeting and during breaks. For the client team member dialing in remotely, the sales team set up a chat so the remote person could interact when they wanted to ask a question or alert the team if they were having trouble hearing the discussion. Every detail contributed to a shared, thoughtful, respectful experience delivered with impact.

For a recent internal meeting, which was very large and virtual, two teams came together from an acquisition. Many people were meeting for the first time. The "director" had an intention of creating one team where everyone felt valued regardless of their legacy company. She asked Company A people to wear blue and Company B people to wear green so it would be immediately clear who was coming from which legacy company. Team members from each company paired up for virtual breakouts to identify something the pair had in common and something they could teach each other based on their various experience. Yes, this is an example of a facilitation technique, but not for cute reasons. The technique was used with strategic intention to create a shared experience.

Public Speaking: It's Hard to Make It Look Easy

Do you have colleagues who seem naturally good at something? They make it look so easy. Maybe they're great at foreign languages, cooking, photography, graphic design, writing, or giving presentations.

I get compliments on my ability to speak and engage a room, and many people think comfort with public speaking is something that comes naturally easily to me. The truth is I have been working on this skill my whole life. My earliest memory onstage is competing in the Little Miss Valley pageant. If there were fifty third-grade girls, I likely ranked forty-nine, just ahead of the girl who tripped on the seam of her long gown and refused to continue.

In fourth grade, I received a smiley face for my speech on the dangers of smoking. At bat again in fifth grade, I got a package of Reese's Cups for winning first place. The topic was the importance of immunizations. In sixth grade, I entered a county-wide competition with the topic of nutrition. I didn't win a thing. I participated in plays and chorus all through high school, from two-bit parts to leading roles. In college, I won awards for theatre.

After college, I received a Master of Fine Arts in acting and performed professionally for many years. As a consulting partner, I gave presentations—too many to count—to colleagues, clients, and recruits. By this time, it was in my DNA. After years and years of working on "You wave your arms too much," I kept the theme going and am now MBA faculty, an award-winning podcast host, and a keynote speaker. I practice new public-speaking skills via video.

Despite working on public speaking for over forty years, I still get nervous. I still get shallow breathing sometimes. I still plant a friend in the audience at times to give me feedback. And just yesterday, I was working on keeping my arms at my sides. It's hard to make public speaking look easy. Embrace what it takes. Contact me if you need help.

Lead in a Pack of Alpha Dogs

> Teamwork is paramount to business success, but teams don't become CEO.

In Alaska's Iditarod, sixteen sled dogs team up to run the grueling race through blistering cold trails from Anchorage to Nome. Every dog in the pack is an alpha dog, both male and female. The musher rotates which dog serves as the lead alpha throughout the course of the race. I studied the Iditarod as a fascinating analogy for business. How do you stand out as an individual high performer while teaming with others just like you?

In the careers I've had, every single one of the people I've been surrounded with has been an overachieving, high-performing, career-driven person. On a normal distribution curve, they're in the top ten percent. They've already self-selected. When you find yourself in this group of people who are all overachiever, type-A personalities, how do you differentiate when you're one of them? You've already been self-selected through the types of jobs you've had, and you're overeducated. Eventually, you find yourself in a little pot together with other type As. How do you lead when you're in a pack of people just like you, when everybody's an alpha dog?

The modern work environment sends mixed messages about what it takes to excel professionally and personally. On one hand, the companies we most admire encourage us to play to our strengths, to be strong team players and collaborators, to take risks, fail fast, and innovate. The entire workplace is filled with amazing, achievement-focused, intelligent people who have been in the upper right-hand tail of the bell curve their entire lives, just like you. Yet, the truth is, although there is no "I" in team, teams do not get the promotion, individuals do. Everyone wants the big bonus allocated only to the top performers. Everyone wants the promotion, but those spots are limited. They're reserved for the alpha dogs.

An alpha is not a growling male dog showing its teeth. An alpha is not the workplace bully. Quite the opposite. Alpha technically means the leader, the lead dog, not the aggressor. Alpha dogs may be male or female. They become the leader of their pack because they are intelligent, intuitive teachers of and caregivers for the other members of the pack, not because they are brute-force dominant or bullies. What leading in a pack of alpha dogs means is best illustrated with the story of the Iditarod.

Each March, the race takes place to honor the Iditarod Trail that ran mail and freight in the gold-mining era. The race was created to commemorate the dogsledding heritage that eroded after the invention of the snowmobile. Up to sixteen dogs can be on a dogsled team, and each team must finish with no fewer than five dogs remaining. 2 weeks. 1000 miles. 35 degrees Fahrenheit. I get cold just thinking about it.

Four positions make up a dogsled team:

1. Leader: the dog at the front of the pack. The fast, intelligent runner at the front of the team who sets the tone and the pace and makes in-the-moment strategic decisions.

2. Swing Dog: second in the phalanx, helping swing the team around turns.

3. Team Dog: all dogs may rotate into this torso position at some point in the race.

4. Wheeler: dogs closest to the 200-pound sled, requiring the most physical strength.

The team dynamics of the Iditarod are fascinating. The leader position rotates based on the strengths required along the changing terrain. The leader may be female or male, and two dogs may share the leader position at times. Each is leading in the pack of alpha dogs to achieve a common goal. The key traits that distinguish the one alpha dog who is a nose above the rest include: best steward of the strategy, most attuned to the needs of the others, and healthiest.

There comes a time in your career when being smart is the price of admission. It used to be that you were often the smartest one in the room. You caught on the quickest. You scored the best. You could figure out anything. You were comfortably top tier on most performance curves. Now, you're surrounded by other people just like you. So how do you differentiate yourself when you look around and see a bunch of yous? You're now in that sphere of your career when characteristics, leadership qualities, emotional intelligence, and creativity start to separate the "really goods" from the "amazings."

There are sixteen attributes (not-so-subtly reflective of the number of Iditarod alpha dogs) that differentiate a Me-Suite leader, an alpha performer, a get-it-done player. You will undoubtedly recognize yourself in each of these characteristics, so high-five for being on the team. But it's not enough to be on the team. You, like the other alphas, have to perform at your best in your current role and be ready for rotation to the next spot on the team. As you go through this list, make note of where you want to raise your game. If you're super strong in an area, think about how to coach others in it. Be real with yourself about in which of these areas you shine and where you need to improve.

Here are the Me-Suite 16:

1. You don't have to have all the answers; you need smart questions. True leaders are constantly curious and confident that they don't have all the answers.
2. Know when to bring in the right person, and do so proudly.
3. Always have a point of view. Your POV is the value you bring in a capsule. The right dose at the right time. Distilled and easy to swallow.
4. Be two steps in front of anticipating others' needs. When you anticipate, you're being strategic; you're in the future.
5. There is no such thing as an informal meeting. Don't mistake casual for half-a$$.
6. Manage up, across, and down.
7. Be able to explain complicated concepts to your grandmother. If you can't, you likely don't truly understand them yourself.
8. Get into personality profiles. They are reliable guides.
9. Know your Achilles's heel. Everybody has one—or two.
10. Communicate, communicate, communicate. This isn't your birthday we're talking about. No one in business likes surprises.
11. People love to give advice. Ask for it more often, and treat it like a gift. Sometimes you'll like it, and sometimes you won't, but always smile and say "thank you."
12. Collaborate. Innovation comes from collaboration, which can be challenging in the remote environment. It's great to consult others for their ideas, but harder to get people together, and sometimes you just want to get the action off your to-do list. Find a way to strike the right balance.
13. Don't say "I." "We" is almost always a more accurate reflection of the way something got accomplished. "I" is only acceptable when taking the blame.

14. Put yourself in the other person's shoes before you send an email, give feedback, or present a recommendation. Try to see the situation from their perspective to tailor your approach.
15. Strike the right tech-touch balance. Don't rely on tech to do all the heavy lifting in your relationships and communications. Do you need to pick up the phone or write a thank-you note by hand, or will a text emoji suffice? Be intentional in your tech-touch choices.
16. Create a personal advisory board of mentors. Just like companies have a board of directors, you need a board as you pursue your own personal goals.

The Iditarod teaches us how to fit in while standing out, how to lead from the front and the back, how to be what your team needs in the moment. Be this type of alpha.

Build Your Personal Board of Directors

Everything I learned about the power of having a personal board of directors, I learned from CEO, board director, and author Ana Dutra. The board of directors of a company selects, supports, and reviews the performance of the CEO. If you are in The Me-Suite running your own life like a company, you are your own CEO. You need a personal board of directors to be a sounding board, a sparring partner, a reality check that you're living up to a Me-Suite mindset. You don't need a *nice* BoD. You need an honest, sincere BoD.

Take these steps to ensure you have the right BoD:

- Define the scope of your BoD. What do you need your board of directors to direct? Do you need a cheerleader or someone to tell you when the baby is ugly? Perhaps you need targeted content expertise. Decide what you really need at this stage, what questions you're wresting with, what goals you want to meet, and be clear about that with yourself and the BoD members.
- Invite individuals who complement your blind spots. You aren't really learning and challenging yourself if there's no diversity of thought. Be cautious about picking close friends. You need advisors, not buddies.
- Target three to four individuals for your BoD. You need a cross-section of perspectives, but a practical size. Invite them individually and personally, sharing your objectives and expectations for the time commitment and how you'll work together.
- Define a timeframe so you and the board members understand the commitment. Six months to one year is both productive and realistic. Setting the duration isn't just about aligning expectations. Confirming the duration provides both parties with a graceful exit when it's time for either to make a change.
- Connect quarterly at a minimum. Without this forced rhythm, you really aren't serious about having a board. Ideally, you'll connect individually with the BoD members. If you choose to host a joint meeting, the collaboration could be very powerful if facilitated sharply.
- Don't get bored with your board. Your Me-Suite needs will change over time. So should your BoD.

WHAT WILL YOU DO DIFFERENTLY ON MONDAY?

ADVICE FROM THE ME-SUITE COMMUNITY

Leading your life with a Me-Suite mindset means you lead with purpose, planning, and power. You lead your own life like C-suites lead the companies we most admire. Just like the C-suite, you marshal your core values, you keep your day-to-day running smoothly, and you stay fresh and relevant for the future you want to have.

The Me-Suite podcast shines a mic on amazing people who lead their own lives with a Me-Suite mindset. Having achieved finalist for Best Business Podcast in 2020 and 2021[43], and ranking among the top two percent of all podcasts globally on ListenNotes[44], the podcast is a forum for high performers to share their core values and examples of how they strive to lead with a Me-Suite mindset. The diverse guests range widely and wildly across ages, from twenty-three to sixty-three, and from start-up

[43] Discover Pods Award 2020, https://awards.discoverpods.com/previous-winners/#2020_Discover_Pods_Winners.
[44] ListenNotes, October 3, 2021, https://www.listennotes.com/podcasts/the-me-suite-donna-peters-okFUD8ln0HA/.

companies to private equity/venture capital and multi-national corporations, holding positions from first-ever jobs to CEOs. The roughly two hundred career-driven and life-minded guests have functions spanning strategy, business development, R&D, manufacturing, supply chain, marketing, finance, procurement, digital/IT, HR, legal, and communications. They represent multiple geographies and varying dimensions of diversity, equity, and inclusion.

At the end of every episode of *The Me-Suite* podcast, I ask my guests, "What's the one thing we can start doing differently on Monday to lead our lives with a Me-Suite mindset?" The morsels of advice are called "Me-Suite suiteners" and span simple, everyday adjustments like, "Order the small, not the large," to deeper reflections, such as, "Discover that thing you uniquely do, and do that thing."

The Me-Suite suiteners are a follower favorite. The following are curated guest verbatims.

Marshal Your Core Values

- Work on yourself first.
- Identify your personal core values, and check in on them quarterly.
- You can find another job; you can't always find another true life partner.
- Tell those you love that you love them.
- Acknowledge the people in your life.
- Reach out to someone you've been meaning to thank.
- Listen to understand others on a fundamental level.
- Be present. Don't multitask your life.
- Don't tie your identity to your company.
- Don't ever give up on friends. Make a friend, and be a friend.
- Invest in your relationships.

- Say no without guilt.
- Define your personal brand promise.
- People rise to your expectations of them.
- Protect what you love to do.
- Decisions determine the quality of our lives.
- Few things truly matter.
- Lead with CARE: communicate, appreciate, respect, engage.
- Surround yourself with people who make you better.
- Feel your feelings; tell your truth; keep your agreements.
- Bring your whole self to all you do.
- Do everything with pride and commitment.
- Eliminate the myth that you don't have time to do what you love.
- If something is truly your priority, you'll find the time.
- Don't make excuses to delay what you want.
- Put people first and everything else falls into place.
- Build trust. If you don't have trust, you don't have much of anything.
- You will have more fun and enjoy more success when you stop trying to get what you want and start helping other people get what they want.
- You're the average of the five people you hang around with.

Keep the Day-to-Day Running Smoothly

- Protect your time.
- Take a pause.
- Life is too short to not have fun.
- Don't mistake kindness for weakness.
- Spend time to get to know the people you work with.
- Create a community of support for others.
- Focus on solving the problem that's creating the problem, not what's right in front of you.
- Solicit feedback, and be grateful when you receive feedback.
- "Keep doing what you're doing" is not acceptable feedback.

- Order the small, not the large.
- Start conversations with big picture questions.
- Create space for colleagues to play with new ideas—create white space.
- Resist the urge to always speak first.
- Speak up and don't hold back.
- Ask, "How can I help you?"
- Recognize you cannot microwave your career. Some things take time.
- Be flexible. Be like water.
- Give yourself permission to lead from where you are.
- Get in where you fit in.
- People want to help people. Ask for help.
- Never lose your ability to be surprised.
- Control the controllables.
- Run your own race.
- Take wonder walks.
- Lead like you're jazz, not classical.
- Appreciate the uniqueness each person brings to the group.
- Any adult eighteen and over needs estate planning.

Stay Fresh and Relevant for the Future You Want to Have

- Do what you love to do.
- Be a mentor, and have a mentor.
- Argue like you're right; listen like you're wrong.
- Acknowledge your weaknesses.
- Get a career coach.
- Think of everything as an iteration. Iterators never fail.
- Shame kills our goals.
- If it's not a 100% yes, then it's a no.
- Ask for what you want.

- Read—a lot.
- Take chances. Step out onto the invisible bridge.
- Be comfortable with being uncomfortable.
- Bring a global mindset to all you do.
- Failure isn't fatal unless you don't learn from it.
- Learn hard things, new topics to see things in new and different ways.
- Do hard things because they are hard.
- Let your career be a mosaic, not a path.
- Never stop learning because life never stops teaching.
- Trust your discontent.
- You need to fail at something to know what you're really made of.
- Options are power. (I had to get mine in there, of course.)

"I still have bigger ambitions. I'm very pleased with what I'm doing, personally and professionally, and at the same time, I want to be something bigger and better than what I am today." –Mike Chapman, Season 3, Episode 10

"Everyone takes something slightly different away from the podcast, and part of the value of The Me-Suite *is not just listening to the twenty minutes, but really processing it, and having a dialogue around how you can apply it to your life." –Donna Sanabria, Season 3, Episode 4*

"Do the work to know what you want. Then, when faced with a decision, if it's not a 'hell yes', then it's a no." –Dr. Lubna Rashid, Season 3, Episode 14

"Keep asking, 'How do I improve?'" –Julien Emery, Season 2, Episode 16

"You need to work at yourself first. Do the core values exercise. Figure out what you stand for, your core values, know what motivates you, what drives you." –Adele Gulfo, Season 1, Episode 38

"Recognize that low self-confidence, at times, is an asset for a leader." –Lisa Finkelstein, Season 2, Episode 23

"When you have a choice, and we all do, choose to be excellent." – Donna Cryer, Season 2, Episode 4

"Control what you can control. If you plan for an exit strategy upfront, you likely won't need an exit strategy." –Guillermo Wasserman, Season 1, Episode 34

"Write the headline you want to see for yourself, and take the leap of faith to achieve it." –Hilal Koc, Season 1, Episode 50

Note: The above are direct excerpts from the episode transcripts of guest interviews, edited for clarity or conciseness.

What do you recommend we do differently on Monday to lead our lives with a Me-Suite mindset? Go to https://www.the-me-suite.com/contact to share your suitener with The Me-Suite community.

YOUR NEXT BEST MOVE

The title of this book spoke to you in some way, and you've read this far. You may now be asking, "What is my next best move? What are my options? Am I intentionally shaping the future I want to have? Am I running *to* something, not *from* something? Is now the time for a coach?"

Most high performers get to this point at some stage in their lives. If you're here now, congratulations. You're among the ranks of those who ask the hard questions and embrace the thoughtful work required to shape the future you want. What smart leaders don't do is try to figure everything out themselves. They also don't rely solely on the advice of their spouse, parents, chaplains, or BFFs. Interestingly, and a bit ironically, those closest to you aren't actually listening closely because they think they already know what you're going to say. It's called the closeness-communication bias. Check out Kate Murphy's *You're Not Listening* for more evidence.

Always be running *to* something, not *from* something.

Another consideration is what you may have already observed in your career climb. It can get lonelier as you rise. A Google search yielded about a million hits on "leadership and loneliness." It's challenging to find people in your regular professional and personal sphere to talk frankly with about your ambitions, hesitations, and wild ideas. Best to enlist an experienced and trained listening ear who can provide truly insightful direction to illuminate your options for what's next.

Anyone performing at an elite level—at anything—has a coach. That's just the truth. Julien Emery, serial entrepreneur, CEO, and former professional hockey player, continually asks, "How do I improve?"[45] Athletes, musicians, actors. Next-generation leaders. CEOs. For these elite performers, the better they are at their craft, the more they

[45] Julien Emery, The Me-Suite podcast, Season 2 Episode 16, https://podcasts.apple.com/us/podcast/keep-asking-how-do-i-improve/id1495889269?i=1000496298763, October 26, 2020.

seek coaching. So why do some high performers too often say, "No, no, I've got this" when offered coaching? Have you ever said this?

If so, ask yourself these questions, and listen honestly to your answers:

- Is now the time to invest in myself?
- Do I have goals, decisions, crossroads that need focus and action?
- Will I progress more meaningfully with an expert in the neuroscience of leadership at my side?

In season 1, episode 25, Chief Strategy Officer Alan Nalle, shares, "My regret is that I should have gotten an executive coach a long time ago." His advice for others on the fence like he had been: "Just jump in."

Coaching helps high performers define and achieve goals. If you're an individual exploring executive coaching for yourself, or a talent leader seeking coaching for your teams, remember the coach-client fit matters. Conduct your due diligence by learning the coach's style, approach, and experience.

When choosing a coach, consider the following questions:

- Does the coach offer a complimentary "discovery call" that allows you to assess fit?
- What are the coach's certifications and experiences?
- Does the coach specialize in the area of your specific goals?
- What is the coach's approach to sessions? Duration, frequency, minimum number, scheduling options, fees, payment terms?
- Does the coach have testimonials and references?

Start by visiting The Me-Suite website for articles, videos, tools, and testimonials at https://www.the-me-suite.com/, and listen to the award-winning podcast, available on all podcast apps.

If your next best move is career and executive coaching, contact me at donna.peters@the-me-suite.com to schedule your complimentary discussion.

ACKNOWLEDGMENTS

I have written this book for five reasons. (As a recovering consultant, I have been trained that lists should be in threes, but this is my book, so the list will have five.)

- About six years ago, I began noticing people quoting my mantra, "Options are power." Executives I had coached over the years were now coaches of others, and they were calling upon my words to guide their next generation of talent. I received requests to speak on the topic almost monthly. I knew something was resonating. In concert, I was receiving nudges from colleagues, like "When are you going to put this in a book?" And so, I am inspired to share.
- I am first and foremost a "Maximizer," in the words of StrengthsFinder. I am drawn to talent. I focus on people's talents to stimulate their excellence. This strength is the foundation of my executive coaching practice today. And so, I am innately driven to share. Of course, I won't name individual clients here, out of respect for our enduring cone of confidentiality. Clients, you know who you are. Thank you for trusting me with your unique stories and your goals. You are the reason.
- I believe no one accomplishes anything alone. The love of my family, the respect and equality in my marriage, my friendships with values-based people, the bosses who took risks on me, the team members who trusted me—all these people played a role in propping me up to the highest levels in a career. I give a special bow of gratitude to all *The Me-Suite* listeners with their shares, likes, downloads, reviews, and referrals. I know who you are, and your generosity brings me to my knees. I was not alone, and so I am fearless to share.
- I humbly recognize that privilege has played a significant role in my achievements. And so, I am grateful to share.

- And then, there's Flo, aka Mom, who gets a special shout-out. Mom was a career professional at a time when most moms didn't have careers; they, arguably, had jobs. I learned from her accountability, loyalty, fairness, and sadly, workplace discrimination. I learned that a woman can be in power without being a bitch, but people may think you're one anyway. I learned that double-income marriages can succeed when you have alignment and respect. Mom told me I had to publish a book in her lifetime, and I always listen to my mother. And so, I am motivated to share.

Thank you, everyone, for surrounding me with your diversity of thoughts and experiences. For being a catalyst, a champion, a nudge, a role model, a mirror, a safe place, a good laugh. Thank you for being you in my life.

ABOUT THE AUTHOR

Donna Peters is a seasoned executive coach, lecturer, and author. As founder of The Me-Suite, Peters helps career-driven professionals shape the life they want to live. Peters believes each of us needs a C-suite mentality to lead our lives with more purpose, planning, and power—like C-suites lead the companies we most admire. Peters knows we each need our version, our own Me-Suite, to marshal our personal core values, keep our day-to-day running smoothly, and stay fresh and relevant for the future we want to have.

As a former senior partner in management consulting, Peters supported the most respected companies in the world with their greatest challenges for twenty years, mobilizing and motivating teams across geographies and functions. She helmed learning, recruiting, and diversity initiatives across North America.

Today, Peters hosts top-ranking podcast *The Me-Suite,* a 2020 and 2021 finalist for Best Business Podcast. She is faculty for the Executive MBA program at Emory University's Goizueta Business School and certified through the International Coaching Federation.

She has been a guest speaker, panelist, and faculty member covering a variety of professional and personal development topics, including "Leading with a Me-Suite Mindset," "The Power of Options," "Leading in a Pack of Alpha Dogs," and "Putting Your Network to Work." She is a frequent contributor to Arianna Huffington's *Thrive Global* community.

As a professional actor earlier in her career, Peters was a company member at Playmakers Repertory Theatre, appeared in George Lucas's *Radioland Murders*, performed her one-woman show, *The Hoffman Hotel*, way-off Broadway, and played the lead in the premier of Joyce Carol Oates's *Bad Girls*. She co-owned a restaurant that won Best of Atlanta with her chef husband and taught English in South Korea. Peters has visited over forty-five countries, gardens with heirloom seeds, and lifts weights religiously.

She holds an MBA with Distinction from Cornell's Johnson School, an MFA in acting from the University of North Carolina-Chapel Hill, an executive coaching diploma from Emory University, and a BA from Davidson College.

Peters's core values are curiosity, freedom, and respect.

www.The-Me-Suite.com

LinkedIn.com/donna-peters-the-me-suite/

Facebook.com/MeSuite

Twitter.com/DonnaPetersCMeO

The Me-Suite podcast is available on all apps.

A Day in My Me-Suite

A Me-Suite follower challenged me to be more transparent about my personal life. While I champion the need to be career-driven and life-minded, this follower felt I wasn't showing enough of Donna, the whole person. So here I share a few random life-minded vignettes.

I garden with the heirloom seed collection I inherited from my father. I am proudest of the green beans and lettuces I coax into becoming dinner. I also hold the trophy for being the only human who killed mint.

I love lifting weights. I dead-lift 185 pounds fifty times each month. With weight-training, I can turn off my brain, and it's the only thing I do truly just for me. It's my time. It's my therapy. It makes me feel invincible.

Husband, Jonathan, is a master chef with an amazing mind. We met thirty-five years ago at college theatre auditions. I asked him out on a date that evening. He got a part in the play. I did not. We have three cats, which is one cat below the CCPI, the crazy cat person index. We don't have children. We were fortunate to have aligned before marriage that we didn't want children. We revisited this decision as I neared forty and decided to stay the course. Knowing how close my mom and I are, I do fear it will be challenging and a bit lonely aging with no children. Maybe I can rent your offspring from the Me-Suite community when that time comes.

Jonathan and I love to travel and have new experiences. Chile, the Galapagos, Iceland, Japan, Peru, and South Africa top our growing list of adventures. That really cold swim with penguins at Fernandina Island. The mesmerizing condors gliding through the thermals of Colca Canyon. The sushi from heaven in Japan. The elephants at midnight crushing trees like matchsticks. Being the sickest we've ever been, downright delirious, beneath the shadow of a stunning snow-capped volcano.

I'm grateful beyond measure for the options life has presented to me all along the way. Options truly are power. The right, not the obligation, to make a change is the most empowering position you can be in. This applies to everything in my life except Jonathan. For the role of life partner, I need no other option.

REVIEW AND SHARE

We live in a world where likes and shares can make a huge impact on others. (I'm specifically referring to the positive type.) Why not impact others by leaving a positive review of this book on your favorite online retailer's website? Just a few words about what you learned here, or how the book has impacted you for the better, could help others find their way to this resource.

Consider making a list of ten colleagues who are poised to step into The Me-Suite and could benefit from this book. Then, share a copy of *Options Are Power*, or direct them to purchase their own copy. You'll be making a deposit in the relationship account by showing you were thinking of them.

Made in USA - Kendallville, IN
92452_9781956642025
02.09.2022 1516